The Words Of The Founders

Our Sacred Natural Rights

&

Our Call To Action

By Paul Rosenberg

Copyright Notices:

To the true Americans:

Those who remain.

Those being born.

Preface

Nothing clarifies a man's thoughts like staking his life on them.

Believe what you will, but when your beliefs deliver death and danger to your door, you'll think again, and hard. This is the moment of truth, when light opinions dissolve and only convictions backed by soul-searching can stand. This is what made the American founders special, and made their thoughts more valuable that the pontifications of subsequent experts and elites: They were forced to risk their lives on their ideas, and the dross was burned away.

Sure, several of these men were exceptionally bright, but no more so than hundreds, or perhaps thousands, of modern Americans. Humanity always produces a certain number of exceptional minds.

In this book you will find approximately 570 thoughts from the American founders, on over 200 subjects, all in their own words. My commentary is minimal and is clearly separated from their words.

I tried not to edit these passages at all. I did update old spellings and I changed some of the archaic words. (For example, I updated "fain" to "gladly," and "felicity" to "happiness.") I also changed some capitalizations. In perhaps a dozen cases I reworded a phrase to clarify it.

Where I thought it would be helpful, I added words to the text in brackets. [Like this.] These bracketed words are either:

> Mine, inserted for the reader's ease of understanding; or,

> words that precede the passage I am quoting.

I added explanatory text in italics, and only in those cases where I thought it was called for.

In almost every case, I have included citations for the quotes, so that they can be verified. In a handful of instances I included quotes that seemed clearly legitimate, for which I had no citation.

The only long section in this book is the one covering Alexander Hamilton. I hadn't planned this, but the need became obvious as the book came together.

For better or worse, the other founders are consistent in nature. They may waver a bit and they may evolve a bit, but Jefferson is always Jefferson and Washington is always Washington. Hamilton is not the same over time, and without illustrating these changes, his writings can be confusing. Furthermore, Hamilton is often at odds with other founders.

Because of this, I found it necessary to spend several pages interweaving quotes and descriptions of the situations in which they arose. As a writer, it is my job to avoid confusing my readers. And in Jefferson's opinion, as well as my own, Hamilton is sometimes confusing on purpose.

Now, with these explanations completed, I present you with the thoughts of the American founders, in their own words. Read them, analyze them, make them your own, and, above all, act upon them. Only then will they stand in the face of danger.

Paul Rosenberg

Contents

Actions

George Washington
Letter to Major-General John Sullivan December 15, 1779
A slender acquaintance with the world must convince every man, that actions, not words, are the true criterion of the attachment of his friends, and that the most liberal professions of good will are very far from being the surest marks of it.

I should be happy that my own experience had afforded fewer examples of the little dependence to be placed upon them.

* * * * *

Benjamin Franklin
Poor Richard's Almanac
Well done is better than well said.

* * * * *

John Adams

Both of these quotes are from Thomas Jefferson, who had a long and sometimes difficult relationship with Adams, as will be examined in the section entitled "Jefferson & Adams."

Thomas Jefferson
Letter to James Madison January 30, 1787
He is vain, irritable, and a bad calculator of the force and probable effect of the motives which govern men.

This is all the ill which can possibly be said of him. He is as disinterested as the Being who made him. He is profound in his views and accurate in his judgment, except where knowledge of the world is necessary to form a judgment. He is so amiable that I pronounce you will love him, if ever you become acquainted with him. He would be, as he was, a great man in Congress.

When Jefferson calls Adams "disinterested," he is using the word in an old way and calling Adams "unbiased and just."

* * * * *

In this case, Jefferson is repeating a comment of Benjamin Franklin that appears often.

Thomas Jefferson
Letter to James Madison July 29, 1789
It [a Presidential title proposed by Adams] is a proof the more of the justice of the character given by Dr. Franklin of my friend:

Always an honest man, often a great one, but sometimes absolutely mad.

* * * * *

America

In his inaugural address, Jefferson lists the felicities (that is, the sources of happiness) that the people of the America found themselves possessing. Note that when talking about "America," the founders usually referred to the land area and its inhabitants, not to a government.

Thomas Jefferson
First Inaugural Address 1801
Kindly separated by nature and a wide ocean from the exterminating havoc of one quarter of the globe; too high-minded to endure the degradations of the others; possessing a chosen country, with room enough for our descendants to the hundredth and thousandth generation; entertaining a due sense of our equal right to the use of our own faculties, to the

acquisitions of our industry, to honor and confidence from our fellow citizens, resulting, not from birth, but from our actions, and their sense of them; enlightened by a benign religion, professed, indeed, and practiced in various forms, yet all of them inculcating honesty, truth, temperance, gratitude, and the love of man; acknowledging and adoring an overruling Providence, which, by all its dispensations, proves that it delights in the happiness of man here and his greater happiness hereafter, -- with all these blessings, what more is necessary to make us a happy and prosperous people?

Still one thing more, fellow-citizens -- a wise and frugal government, which shall restrain men from injuring one another, which shall leave them otherwise free to regulate their own pursuits of industry and improvement, and shall not take from the mouth of labor the bread it has earned. This is the sum of good government, and this is necessary to close the circle of our felicities.

* * * * *

Americans

Here Samuel Adams describes the spirit of the people who preserved freedom in America. Note the dates: All of these comments are made before the Boston Tea Party, the Declaration of Independence and the Revolutionary War.

Samuel Adams
Boston Gazette, January 21, 1771
Nothing, in my opinion, can convey a more unjust idea of the spirit of a true American, than to suppose he would even compliment, much less make an adulating address to any person sent here to trample on the Rights of his Country; or that he would ever condescend to kiss the hand which is ready prepared to rivet his own fetters.

"Fetters" are shackles and chains.

* * * * *

Samuel Adams

Boston Gazette, September 9, 1771

Perhaps there never was a people who discovered themselves more strongly attached to their natural and constitutional rights and liberties, than the British Colonists on this American Continent - Their united and successful struggles against that slavery with which they were threatened by the stamp-act, will undoubtedly be recorded by future historians to their immortal honor.

This reference to "constitutional rights" is to the Constitution of The United Kingdom, and probably to the Bill of Rights of 1689 in particular.

"Natural rights" refers to the formulation of John Locke, that all men are naturally in "a state of perfect freedom to order their actions, and dispose of their possessions and persons as they think fit, within the bounds of the law of Nature, without asking leave or depending upon the will of any other man."

* * * * *

Samuel Adams

Boston Gazette, September 16, 1771

That union of the colonies in their common danger, by which they became powerful, was the occasion of the greatest perplexity to their enemies on both sides the Atlantic; and it has been ever since their constant endeavor by all manner of arts to destroy it.

In this, it must be confessed, they have discovered an unanimity, zeal and perseverance, worthy to be imitated by those who are embarked in the cause of American freedom. It is by united councils, a steady zeal, and a manly fortitude, that this continent must expect to recover its violated rights and liberties.

* * * * *

Samuel Adams

Letter to Richard Henry Lee April 10, 1773

This Province, and this Town especially, have suffered a great Share of Ministerial Wrath and Insolence: But God be thanked, there is, I trust, a Spirit prevailing, which will never submit to Slavery.

The Compliance of New York in making annual Provision for a military Force designed to carry Acts of Tyranny into Execution: The Timidity of some Colonies and the Silence of others is discouraging: But the active Vigilance, the manly Generosity and the Steady Perseverance of Virginia and South Carolina, gives us Reason to hope, that the Fire of true Patriotism will at length spread throughout the Continent; the consequence of which must be the acquisition of all we wish for.

* * * * *

Arguing

Franklin explains his experiences with arguing and contention, and why it is a bad habit.

Benjamin Franklin
His Autobiography, 1771

There was another bookish lad in the town, John Collins by name, with whom I was intimately acquainted. We sometimes disputed, and very fond we were of argument, and very desirous of confuting one another, which disputatious turn, by the way, is apt to become a very bad habit, making people often extremely disagreeable in company by the contradiction that is necessary to bring it into practice; and thence, besides souring and spoiling the conversation, is productive of disgusts and, perhaps enmities where you may have occasion for friendship. I had caught it by reading my father's books of dispute about religion.

Persons of good sense, I have since observed, seldom fall into it, except lawyers, university men, and men of all sorts that have been bred at Edinborough.

* * * * *

Arms

Many of the quotes related to the keeping and bearing of arms that currently circulate are poorly referenced and sometimes altered. Nonetheless, the founders were in generally favor of an armed populace and here are a few quotes that display this:

Thomas Jefferson
Jefferson's Literary Commonplace Book
Laws that forbid the carrying of arms ... disarm only those who are neither inclined nor determined to commit crimes. ... Such laws make things worse for the assaulted and better for the assailants; they serve rather to encourage than to prevent homicides, for an unarmed man may be attacked with greater confidence than an armed man.

* * * * *

Thomas Jefferson
Draft Constitution for Virginia June 1776
No freeman shall be debarred the use of arms [within his own lands].

* * * * *

Thomas Jefferson
Letter to John Cartwright, 1824
The constitutions of most of our States assert that all power is inherent in the people; that they may exercise it by themselves... that it is their right and duty to be at all times armed.

* * * * *

The Assumption

The Assumption of state debts was a huge issue and scandal in its day, fraught with lies, disagreements, back room deals and fraud. Here, Jefferson recounts the story of how it happened.

Thomas Jefferson
Letter to an unknown recipient. 1793

The Assumption of the State debts in 1790 was a supplementary measure in Hamilton's fiscal system. When attempted in the House of Representatives it failed. This threw Hamilton himself, and a number of members into deep dismay. Going to the President's one day I met Hamilton, as I approached the door. His look was somber, haggard, and dejected beyond description; even his dress uncouth and neglected. He asked to speak with me.

He stood in the street near the door; he opened the subject of the Assumption of the State debts, the necessity of it in the general fiscal arrangement, and its indispensable necessity towards a preservation of the Union; and particularly of the New England States, who had made great expenditures during the war on expeditions which, though of their own undertaking, were for the common cause: that they considered the Assumption of these by the Union so just, and its denial so probably injurious that they would make it a sine qua non of [utterly necessary for] a continuance of the Union. That as to his own part, if he had not credit enough to carry such a measure as that, he could be of no use and was determined to resign.

He observed at the same time, that though our particular business lay in separate departments [Jefferson Secretary of State and Hamilton Secretary of Treasury], yet the administration and its success was a common concern, and that we should make common cause in supporting one another.

He added his wish that I would interest my friends from the South, who were those most opposed to it. I answered that I had been so long absent from my country [as Ambassador to France] that I had lost a familiarity with its affairs, and being but lately returned had not yet got into the train of them; that the fiscal system being out of my department I had not yet undertaken to consider and understand it; that the Assumption had struck me in an unfavorable light, but still, not having considered it sufficiently, I had not concerned [myself] in it, but that I would revolve what he had urged in my mind.

It was a real fact that the Eastern and Southern members (South Carolina however was with the former) had got into the most extreme ill humor with one another. This broke out on every question with the most alarming heat; the bitterest animosity seemed to be engendered, and though they met every day, little or nothing could be done from mutual distrust and antipathy.

On considering the situation of things, I thought the first step towards some conciliation of views would be to bring Mr. Madison and Colonel Hamilton to a friendly discussion of the subject. I immediately wrote to each to come and dine with me the next day, mentioning that we should be alone, that the object was to find some temperament for the present fever, and that I was persuaded that men of sound heads and honest views needed nothing more than explanation and mutual understanding to enable them to unite in some measures which might enable us to get along.

They came; I opened the subject to them, acknowledged that my situation had not permitted me to understand it sufficiently but encouraged them to consider the thing together. They did so. It ended in Mr. Madison's acquiescence in a proposition that the question should be again brought before the House by way of amendment from the Senate: that though he would not vote for it, nor entirely withdraw his opposition, yet he should not be strenuous but leave it to its fate.

It was observed, I forget by which of them, that as the pill would be a bitter one to the Southern States, something should be done to soothe them; that the removal of the seat of government to the Potomac was a just measure, and would probably be a popular one with them, and would be a proper one to follow the Assumption. It was agreed to speak to Mr. White and Mr. Lee whose districts lay on the Potomac, and to refer to them to consider how far the interests of their particular districts might be a sufficient inducement in them to yield to the Assumption. This was done. Lee came into it without hesitation: Mr. White had some qualms but finally agreed.

The measure came down by way of amendment from the Senate and was finally carried by the change of White and Lee's votes. But the removal to the Potomac could not be carried unless Pennsylvania could be engaged in it. This Hamilton took on himself, and chiefly, as I understood, through the agency of Robert Morris, obtained a vote of that State, on agreeing to an intermediate residence at Philadelphia.

This is the real history of the Assumption, about which many erroneous conjectures have been published. It was unjust in itself, oppressive to the States, and was acquiesced to merely from a fear of discussion.

While our government was still in its most infant state, it enabled Hamilton so to strengthen himself by corrupt services to many, so that he could afterwards carry his bank scheme and every measure he proposed in defiance of all opposition.

In fact, it was a principal ground whereon was reared up that speculating phalanx, in and out of Congress, which has since been able to give laws to change the political complexion of the government of the United States.

These last two paragraphs are powerful indictments of Hamilton. This will be examined further in the section entitled "Alexander Hamilton."

* * * * *

Madison notes that there were problems both before and after the Assumption. Also that the many had become victims to the few.

James Madison
Letter to Thomas Jefferson August 8, 1791
These and other abuses make it a problem whether the system of the old paper under a bad government or of the new under a good one be chargeable with the greater substantial injustice. The true difference seems to be that by the former the few were the victims to the many, by the latter the many to the few.

＊ ＊ ＊ ＊ ＊

Authenticity

Benjamin Franklin
Poor Richard's Almanac
What you would seem to be, be really.

＊ ＊ ＊ ＊ ＊

Benjamin Franklin
Poor Richard's Almanac
It's common for Men to give [many] pretended Reasons instead of one real one.

＊ ＊ ＊ ＊ ＊

Authority

Sam Adams rejects obedience to authority and faith in great men:

Samuel Adams
Boston Gazette, August 20, 1770

It is enough for those who are dependent upon the great for commissions, pensions, and the like, to preach up implicit faith in the great.

Others whose minds are unfettered will think for themselves. They will not blindly adopt the opinions even of persons who are advanced to the first stations in the courts of law and equity, any further than the reasons which they expressly give are convincing. They will judge freely of every point of state doctrine, & reject with disdain a blind submission to the authority of mere names, as being equally ridiculous, as well as dangerous in government and religion.

* * * * *

Banks

In these passages, Jefferson refers to fractional reserve and central banking. The crucial issue was that these types of banking involve monopoly rights to create money with a stroke of a pen, creating a small, hyper-empowered class. The primary alternative to this arrangement is the use of silver and gold as money. This was disliked by bankers and financiers for a variety of reasons, among them that gold and silver cannot be created on demand.

Note that "circulating medium" is whatever is commonly used as money (including paper notes, but usually silver and/or gold coins.). "Specie" refers to gold and silver coins.

Note also that properly, "money" is something that has inherent value (as gold or silver) and "currency" is either a receipt for money or a substitute for money.

Thomas Jefferson

Letter to John Taylor, 1816

I sincerely believe, with you, that banking institutions are more dangerous than standing armies.

* * * * *

Thomas Jefferson

Letter to John W. Eppes, 1813

Bank paper must be suppressed, and the circulating medium must be restored to the nation to whom it belongs.

* * * * *

Thomas Jefferson

Letter to Albert Gallatin December 13, 1803

I observe an idea of establishing a branch bank of the United States in New Orleans. This institution is one of the most deadly hostility existing against the principles and form of our Constitution.

The nation is at this time so strong and united in its sentiments that it cannot be shaken at this moment. But suppose a series of unfortunate events should occur sufficient to bring into doubt the competency of a republican government to meet a crisis of great danger, or to unhinge the confidence of the people in the public functionaries; an institution like this, penetrating by its branches every part of the union, acting by command and in phalanx may, in a critical moment, upset the government.

I deem no government safe which is under the vassalage of any self-constituted authorities, or any other authority than that of the nation or its regular functionaries. What an obstruction could not this Bank of the United States, with al its branch banks, be in time of war! It might dictate to us the peace we should accept, or withdraw its aids. Ought we then to give further growth to an institution so powerful, so hostile?

"Vassalage" meant "in dependence or servitude to."

Thomas Jefferson
Letter to Abbe Salimankis 1810
That we are overdone with banking institutions which have banished the precious metals and substituted a more fluctuating and unsafe medium, that these have withdrawn capital from useful improvements and employments to nourish idleness, that the wars of the world have swollen our commerce beyond the wholesome limits of exchanging our own productions for our own wants, and that, for the emolument of a small proportion of our society who prefer these demoralizing pursuits to labors useful to the whole, the peace of the whole is endangered and all our present difficulties produced, are evils more easily to be deplored than remedied.

* * * * *

Thomas Jefferson
Letter to Thomas Cooper 1814
Everything predicted by the enemies of banks, in the beginning, is now coming to pass. We are to be ruined now by the deluge of bank paper. It is cruel that such revolutions in private fortunes should be at the mercy of avaricious adventurers, who, instead of employing their capital, if any they have, in manufactures, commerce, and other useful pursuits, make it an instrument to burden all the interchanges of property with their swindling profits, profits which are the price of no useful industry of theirs.

* * * * *

Here Jefferson argues for an alternative to the central bank, and for the re-introduction of gold and silver.

Thomas Jefferson
Letter to Thomas Cooper 1814
Necessity, as well as patriotism and confidence, will make us all eager to receive treasury notes, if founded on specific taxes. Congress may borrow of the public, and without interest, all the money they may want, to the amount of a

competent circulation, by merely issuing their own promissory notes, of proper denominations for the larger purposes of circulation, but not for the small. Leave that door open for the entrance of metallic money.

* * * * *

Thomas Jefferson
Letter to John Wayles Eppes November 16, 1813
It is a palpable falsehood to say we can have specie for our paper whenever demanded. Instead, then, of yielding to the cries of scarcity of medium set up by speculators, projectors and commercial gamblers, no endeavors should be spared to begin the work of reducing it by such gradual means as may give time to private fortunes to preserve their poise, and settle down with the subsiding medium; and that, for this purpose, the States should be urged to concede to the General Government, with a saving of chartered rights, the exclusive power of establishing banks of discount for paper.

* * * * *

Again, Jefferson proposes routes around the banking system.

Thomas Jefferson
Letter to Albert Gallatin, 1803
In order to be able to meet a general combination of the banks against us in a critical emergency, could we not make a beginning towards an independent use of our own money, towards holding our own bank in all the deposits where it is received, and letting the treasurer give his draft or note for payment at any particular place, which, in a well-conducted government, ought to have as much credit as any private draft or bank note or bill, and would give us the same facilities which we derive from the banks?

* * * * *

Bankers

Thomas Jefferson
Letter to Josephus B. Stuart, 1817
The bank mania...is raising up a moneyed aristocracy in our country which has already set the government at defiance.

* * * * *

The Bill Of Rights

The Constitution almost certainly would have been rejected without the Bill of Rights. Below, Madison acknowledges this fact, Jefferson agrees, and Hamilton argues against the Bill of Rights.

It is important to understand that the American Bill of Rights is inaccurately named – the ten amendments are things that Congress is forbidden to do, not a list of Rights. All Rights are inherently resident in the people and cannot be given to them by any king, council or legislature.

James Madison
I believe that the great mass of the people who opposed [the Constitution], disliked it because it did not contain effectual provision against encroachments on particular rights.

* * * * *

Thomas Jefferson
Letter to F. Hopkinson March 13, 1789
What I disapproved from the first moment also, was the lack of a bill of rights, to guard liberty against the legislative as well as the executive branches of the government; that is to say, to secure freedom in religion, freedom of the press, freedom from monopolies, freedom from unlawful imprisonment, freedom from a permanent military, and a trial by jury in all cases determinable by the laws of the land. I disapproved also

the perpetual re-eligibility of the President. To these points of disapprobation I adhere.

Alexander Hamilton
Federalist #84

It has been several times truly remarked that bills of rights are, in their origin, stipulations between kings and their subjects, abridgements of prerogative in favor of privilege, reservations of rights not surrendered to the prince. Such was Magna Charta, obtained by the barons, sword in hand, from King John. Such were the subsequent confirmations of that charter by succeeding princes. Such was the Petition Of Right assented to by Charles I., in the beginning of his reign. Such, also, was the Declaration of Right presented by the Lords and Commons to the Prince of Orange in 1688, and afterwards thrown into the form of an act of parliament called the Bill of Rights.

It is evident, therefore, that, according to their primitive signification, they have no application to constitutions professedly founded upon the power of the people, and executed by their immediate representatives and servants.

Here, in strictness, the people surrender nothing; and as they retain every thing they have no need of particular reservations. "We, The People of the United States, to secure the blessings of liberty to ourselves and our posterity, do Ordain and Establish this Constitution for the United States of America." Here is a better recognition of popular rights, than volumes of those aphorisms which make the principal figure in several of our State bills of rights, and which would sound much better in a treatise of ethics than in a constitution of government.

Hamilton is right, of course, regarding the English Bills of Rights. The document we refer to as the Bill of Rights, however – the same one that was in question in 1788 – was of a wholly different character, as mentioned in the opening note to this section. Hamilton ignores this crucial difference, although he certainly understood it.

* * * * *

Books, Reading

Reading, an utterly crucial activity, was of immense importance to the founders, and they commented upon it widely.

George Washington
Letter to Jonathan Boucher, July 9, 1771
I conceive a knowledge of books is the basis upon which other knowledge is to be built.

* * * * *

George Washington
Letter to George Washington Parke Custis, November 13, 1796
Light reading, by this, I mean books of little importance, may amuse for the moment, but leaves nothing solid behind.

* * * * *

Thomas Jefferson
Letter to Alexander Donald February 7, 1788
I had rather be shut up in a very modest cottage with my books, my family and a few old friends, dining on simple bacon, and letting the world roll on as it liked, than to occupy the most splendid post, which any human power can give.

* * * * *

Thomas Jefferson
Letter to John Adams June 10, 1815
I cannot live without books.

* * * * *

John Adams

Letter to his wife December 28, 1794

I read my eyes out and can't read half enough. ... The more one reads the more one sees we have to read.

* * * * *

Benjamin Franklin

His Autobiography, 1771

From a child I was fond of reading, and all the little money that came into my hands was ever laid out in books.

Pleased with the Pilgrim's Progress, my first collection was of John Bunyan's works in separate little volumes. I afterward sold them to enable me to buy R. Burton's Historical Collections; they were small chapmen's books, and cheap, 40 or 50 in all.

My father's little library consisted chiefly of books in polemic divinity, most of which I read, and have since often regretted that, at a time when I had such a thirst for knowledge, more proper books had not fallen in my way since it was now resolved I should not be a clergyman.

Plutarch's Lives was there, in which I read abundantly, and I still think that time spent to great advantage. There was also a book of De Foe's, called an Essay on Projects, and another of Dr. Mather's, called Essays to do Good, which perhaps gave me a turn of thinking that had an influence on some of the principal future events of my life.

* * * * *

The Boston Tea Party

The Boston Tea Party has stood for more than two centuries as a pivotal moment in American history. Few, however, know any more than the barest details. Here is a direct account of the event from Samuel Adams, who was fully involved:

Samuel Adams
Letter to Arthur Lee Dec. 31, 1773

My Dear Sir, I am now to inform you of as remarkable an event as had yet happened since the commencement of our struggle for American liberty. The meeting of the town of Boston, an account of which I enclosed in my last, was succeeded by the arrival of the ship Falmouth, Captain Hall, with 114 chests of the East India Company's tea, on the 28th of November last.

The next day the people met in Faneuil hall, without observing the rules prescribed by law for calling them together; and although that hall is capable of holding 1200 or 1300 men, they were soon obliged for the want of room to adjourn to the Old South meeting-house; where were assembled upon this important occasion 5000, some say 6000 men, consisting of the respectable inhabitants of this and the adjacent towns.

The business of the meeting was conducted with decency, unanimity, and spirit. Their resolutions you will observe in an enclosed printed paper. It naturally fell upon the correspondence for the town of Boston to see that these resolutions were carried into effect. This committee, finding that the owner of the ship after she was unloaded of all her cargo except the tea, was by no means disposed to take the necessary steps for her sailing back to London, thought it best to call in the committees of Charlestown, Cambridge, Brookline, Roxbury, and Dorchester, all of which towns are in the neighborhood of this, for their advice and assistance. After a free conference and due consideration, they dispersed.

The next day, being the 14th, inst. the people met again at the Old South church, and having ascertained the owner, they compelled him to apply at the custom house for a clearance for his ship to London with the tea on board, and appointed ten gentlemen to see it performed; after which they adjourned till Thursday the 16th. The people then met, and Mr. Rotch informed them that he had according to their injunction applied to the collector of the customs for a clearance, and received in answer from the collector that he could not consistently with his duty grant him a clearance, until the ship should be discharged of the dutiable article on board.

It must be here observed that Mr. Rotch had before made a tender of the tea to the consignees, being told by them that it was not practicable for them at that time to receive the tea, by reason of a constant guard kept upon it by armed men; but that when it might be practicable, they would receive it. He demanded the captain's bill of lading and the freight, both which they refused him, against which he entered a regular protest. The people then required Mr. Rotch to protest the refusal of the collector to grant him a clearance under these circumstances, and thereupon to wait upon the governor for a permit to pass the castle in her voyage to London, and then adjourned till the afternoon. They then met, and after waiting till sun-setting, Mr. Rotch returned, and acquainted them that the governor had refused to grant him a passport, thinking it inconsistent with the laws and his duty to the king, to do it until the ship should be qualified, notwithstanding Mr. Rotch had acquainted him with the circumstances above mentioned.

You will observe by the printed proceedings, that the people were resolved that the tea should not be landed, but sent back to London in the same bottom; and the property should be safe guarded while in port, which they punctually performed. It cannot therefore be fairly said that the destruction of the property was in their contemplation. It is proved that the consignees, together with the collector of the customs, and the governor of the province, prevented the safe return of the East India Company's property (the danger of the sea only excepted) to London. The people finding all their endeavors for this purpose thus totally frustrated, dissolved the meeting, which had consisted by common estimation of at least seven thousand men, many of whom had come from towns at the distance of twenty miles.

In less than four hours every chest of tea on board three ships which had by this time arrived, three hundred and forty-two chests, or rather the contents of them, was thrown into the sea, without the least injury to the vessels or any other property. The only remaining vessel which was expected with this detested article, is by the act of righteous heaven cast on shore on the back of Cape Cod, which has often been the sad fate of many a more valuable cargo.

For a more particular detail of facts, I refer you to our worthy friend, Dr. Hugh Williamson, who kindly takes the charge of this letter. We have had great pleasure in his company for a few weeks past; and he favored the meeting with his presence.

You cannot imagine the height of joy that sparkles in the eyes and animates the countenances as well as the hearts of all we meet on this occasion; excepting the disappointed, disconcerted Hutchinson and his tools. I repeat what I wrote you in my last; if lord Dartmouth has prepared his plan let him produce it speedily; but his lordship must know that it must be such a plan as will not barely amuse, much less farther irritate but conciliate the affection of the inhabitants.

I had forgot to tell you that before the arrival of either of these ships, the tea commissioners had preferred a petition to the governor and council, praying "to resign themselves and the property in their care, to his Excellency and the board as guardians and protectors of the people, and that measures may be directed for the landing and securing the tea," &c. I have enclosed you the result of the council on that petition. He (the governor) is now, I am told, consulting his lawyers and books to make out that the resolves of the meeting are treasonable.

* * * * *

John Adams
December 17, 1773

This is the most magnificent movement of all! There is a dignity, a majesty, a sublimity, in this last effort of the patriots that I greatly admire. The people should never rise without doing something to be remembered — something notable and striking. This destruction of the tea is so bold, so daring, so firm, intrepid and inflexible, and it must have so important consequences, and so lasting, that I can't but consider it as an epoch in history!

* * * * *

Calvinism

John Calvin was a theologian in Geneva, Switzerland, during the middle of the 16th Century. His teachings involved five primary points. Among them were these:

- *The total depravity of man: You are not capable of choosing to do good.*

- *Unconditional election. You are predestined for heaven or hell, and there is nothing you can do about it either way.*

With these teachings, Jefferson found fault:

Thomas Jefferson
Letter to John Adams April 11, 1823

I can never join Calvin in addressing his god. He was indeed an Atheist, which I can never be; or rather his religion was Daemonism. If ever man worshipped a false god, he did. The being described in his 5 points is not the God whom you and I acknowledge and adore, the Creator and benevolent governor of the world; but a daemon of malignant spirit. It would be more pardonable to believe in no god at all, than to blaspheme him by the atrocious attributes of Calvin.

Indeed I think that every Christian sect gives a great handle to Atheism by their general dogma that, without a revelation, there would not be sufficient proof of the being of a god.

Centralization, Decentralization

Centralization was a crucial issue to the founders. Strong arguments for and against it began with the new Constitution in 1787 and continued long after ratification.

In general, the state leaders who lost personal power to the new national government took it well. But the more philosophical and principled of the founders (especially Jefferson) saw great danger in centralization. They accepted the Constitution as a necessary compromise, but remained opposed to the principle of centralization and spoke against it consistently.

In this first quote, Adams discusses the removing of information and input from the assembly and people of Massachusetts, and consolidating it in the Governor alone. In other words, the centralizing of power.

Samuel Adams
Letter to Stephen Sayre. November 16, 1770
I must mention to you that the Minister has taken a Method which in my Opinion has a direct tendency to set up a despotism here, or rather is the thing itself--and that is by sending Instructions to the Governor to be the rule of his Administration & forbidding him as the Governor declares to make them known to us, the Design of which may be to prevent his ever being made responsible for any measures he may advise in order to introduce & establish arbitrary power over the Colonies.

* * * * *

Jefferson's decentralization principle, probably the most commonly expressed principle of his later years:

Thomas Jefferson
Autobiography, 1821
It is not by the consolidation or concentration, of powers, but by their distribution that good government is effected.

* * * * *

Thomas Jefferson

Letter to William Johnson, 1822

They [the republican party] rally to the point which they think next best, a consolidated government. Their aim is now, therefore, to break down the rights reserved by the Constitution to the States as a bulwark against that consolidation, the fear of which produced the whole of the opposition to the Constitution at its birth...

I trust... that the friends of the real Constitution and Union will prevail against consolidation, as they have done against monarchism. I scarcely know myself which is most to be deprecated, a consolidation, or dissolution of the States. The horrors of both are beyond the reach of human foresight.

The republican party Jefferson mentions above has no relation to the Republican party of modern times.

A "bulwark" is a defensive wall.

* * * * *

Thomas Jefferson

Letter to William T. Berry, 1822

We already see the power [of the judiciary], installed for life, responsible to no authority (for impeachment is not even a scare-crow), advancing with a noiseless and steady pace to the great object of consolidation.

The foundations are already deeply laid by their decisions for the annihilation of constitutional State rights, and the removal of every check, every counterpoise to the engulfing power of which themselves are to make a sovereign part.

If ever this vast country is brought under a single government, it will be one of the most extensive corruption, indifferent and incapable of a wholesome care over so wide a spread of surface.

* * * * *

Thomas Jefferson
Letter to C.W. Gooch, 1826
Although I have little hope that the torrent of consolidation can be withstood, I should not be for giving up the ship without efforts to save her. She lived well through the first squall, and may weather the present one.

The "first squall" Jefferson refers to was the centralization of power under the Federalists between 1790 and 1800.

* * * * *

Thomas Jefferson
Letter to Samuel Johnson, 1823
I have been criticized for saying that a prevalence of the doctrines of consolidation would one day call for reformation or revolution.

* * * * *

Thomas Jefferson
Letter to William B. Giles, 1825
I see with the deepest affliction, the rapid strides with which the Federal branch of our government is advancing towards the usurpation of all the rights reserved to the States, and the consolidation in itself of all powers, foreign and domestic; and that too, by constructions which, if legitimate, leave no limits to their power.

* * * * *

During this period of history the Industrial Revolution, with its large economies of scale (which tended toward centralization) was spreading across America. This is Jefferson's plan for a practical, decentralized system under those conditions, almost thirty years after the Constitution was written:

Thomas Jefferson
Letter to Samuel Kerchival, 1816
The article, nearest my heart, is the division of counties into wards. These will be pure and elementary republics, the sum

of all which, taken together, composes the State, and will make of the whole a true democracy as to the business of the wards, which is that of nearest and daily concern.

The affairs of the larger sections, of counties, of States, and of the Union, not admitting personal transactions by the people, will be delegated to agents elected by themselves; and representation will thus be substituted, where personal action becomes impracticable.

Yet, even over these representative organs, should they become corrupt and perverted, the division into wards constituting the people, in their wards, a regularly organized power, enables them by that organization to crush, regularly and peaceably, the usurpations of their unfaithful agents, and rescues them from the dreadful necessity of doing it insurrectionally.

In this way we shall be as republican as a large society can be; and secure the continuance of purity in our government, by the salutary, peaceable, and regular control of the people.

In the last line, Jefferson (using an old order of wording) does not refer to the government controlling the people, but the people controlling the government.

* * * * *

Character

Here the great man of character, George Washington, speaks of his own. Notice that these statements are made when he was twenty-five years old. He spoke less about himself in later years. Even if we regard these statements as a young man's boasts, we see clearly what he was striving to become.

George Washington
Letter to the Earl of Loudoun, March, 1757
My nature is open and honest and free from guile.

* * * * *

George Washington

Letter to Governor Robert Dinwiddie August 27, 1757

It is with pleasure I receive reproof, when reproof is due, because no person can be readier to accuse me, than I am to acknowledge an error, when I am guilty of one; nor more desirous of atoning for a crime, when I am sensible of having committed it.

"Crime" is not used in a literal sense here, but as in making an error.

* * * * *

The Character of Candidates

Sam Adams is firmly convinced that the consideration of a man's general character is crucial in the analysis of any political candidate.

Samuel Adams

Loyalty and Sedition, The Advertiser, 1748

He therefore is the truest friend to the liberty of his country who tries most to promote its virtue, and who, so far as his power and influence extend, will not suffer a man to be chosen into any office of power and trust who is not a wise and virtuous man.

We must not conclude merely upon a man's haranguing upon liberty, and using the charming sound, that he is fit to be trusted with the liberties of his country. It is not unfrequent to hear men declaim loudly upon liberty, who, if we may judge by the whole tenor of their actions, mean nothing else by it but their own liberty.

* * * * *

John Adams

Dissertation on Canon and Feudal Law, 1765

Liberty cannot be preserved without a general knowledge among the people, who have a right, from the frame of their nature, to knowledge, as their great Creator, who does nothing in vain, has given them understandings, and a desire to know.

But besides this, they have a right, an indisputable, unalienable, indefeasible, divine right to that most dreaded and envied kind of knowledge; I mean, of the characters and conduct of their rulers.

* * * * *

Charisma

Benjamin Franklin
Poor Richard's Almanack 1735
Here comes the orator! With his flood of words and his drop of reason.

* * * * *

Child-Rearing

Benjamin Franklin
His Autobiography, 1771
At [my father's] table he liked to have, as often as he could, some sensible friend or neighbor to converse with, and always took care to start some ingenious or useful topic for discourse, which might tend to improve the minds of his children.

By this means he turned our attention to what was good, just, and prudent in the conduct of life; and little or no notice was ever taken of what related to the food on the table, whether it was well or ill prepared, in or out of season, of good or bad flavor, preferable or inferior to this or that other thing of the kind, so that I was brought up in such a perfect inattention to those matters as to be quite indifferent what kind of food was set before me, and so unobservant of it, that to this day if I am asked I can scarce tell a few hours after dinner what I dined upon.

* * * * *

Christianity

Christianity was the great central set of ideas in early American. Various groups interpreted them differently and non-Christians were accepted, but no other group of ideas was remotely as influential.

Benjamin Franklin
Letter to the French ministry, March, 1778
Whoever shall introduce into public affairs the principles of primitive Christianity will change the face of the world.

* * * * *

This quote from John Adams demonstrates the change in sentiments that was occurring in the 1750s. This was the moment when Adams says that the revolution really occurred. (See his quote listed under "The Revolution.")

John Adams
Diary entry, February 18, 1756
Spent an hour in the beginning of the evening at Major Gardiner's, where it was thought that the design of Christianity was not to make men good riddle-solvers, or good mystery-mongers, but good men, good magistrates, and good subjects, good husbands and good wives, good parents and good children, good masters and good servants.

The following questions may be answered some time or other, namely, - Where do we find a precept in the Gospel requiring Ecclesiastical Synods? Convocations? Councils? Decrees? Creeds? Confessions? Oaths? Subscriptions? and whole cart-loads of other trumpery that we find religion encumbered with in these days?

Thomas Jefferson

Letter to Benjamin Rush April 12, 1803

To the corruptions of Christianity I am indeed opposed; but not to the genuine precepts of Jesus himself. I am a Christian, in the only sense he wished any one to be; sincerely attached to his doctrines, in preference to all others; ascribing to himself every human excellence; and believing he never claimed any other.

* * * * *

Thomas Jefferson

The Anas February 1, 1800

When the clergy addressed General Washington on his departure from the government, it was observed in their consultation that he had never on any occasion said a word to the public which showed a belief in the Christian religion and they thought they should so pen their address as to force him at length to declare publicly whether he was a Christian or not. They did so. However [Dr. Rush] observed [that] the old fox was too cunning for them. He answered every article of their address particularly except that, which he passed over without notice. Rush observes he never did say a word on the subject in any of his public papers except in his valedictory letter to the Governors of the states when he resigned his commission in the army, wherein he speaks of the benign influence of the Christian religion.

* * * * *

Here, Franklin expresses his appreciation of religion as a public exercise, and his preference for the Christian religion. (Also see Franklin's quotes listed under "Deism.")

Benjamin Franklin

Proposals Relating to the Education of Youth in Pennsylvania 1749

History will also afford frequent opportunities of showing the necessity of a Public Religion, from its usefulness to the public; the advantage of a religious character among private Persons; the mischiefs of superstition, etc. and the excellence of the Christian Religion above all others ancient or modern.

* * * * *

Patrick Henry
Last Will and Testament November 20, 1798
This is all the inheritance I can give my dear family. The religion of Christ can give them one which will make them rich indeed.

* * * * *

Church Attendance

Benjamin Franklin
His Autobiography, 1774
Though' I seldom attended any public worship, I had still an opinion of its propriety, and of its utility when rightly conducted, and I regularly paid my annual subscription for the support of the only Presbyterian minister or meeting we had in Philadelphia.

He used to visit me sometimes as a friend, and admonish me to attend his administrations, and I was now and then prevailed on to do so, once for five Sundays successively.

Had he been in my opinion a good preacher, perhaps I might have continued, notwithstanding the occasion I had for the Sunday's leisure in my course of study; but his discourses were chiefly either polemic arguments, or explications of the peculiar doctrines of our sect, and were all to me very dry, uninteresting, and unedifying, since not a single moral principle was inculcated or enforced, their aim seeming to be rather to make us Presbyterians than good citizens.

At length he took for his text that verse of the fourth chapter of Philippians, "Finally, brethren, whatsoever things are true, honest, just, pure, lovely, or of good report, if there be any virtue, or any praise, think on these things." And I imagined, in a sermon on such a text, we could not miss of having some morality.

But he confined himself to five points only, as meant by the apostle, these were.: 1. Keeping holy the Sabbath day. 2. Being diligent in reading the holy Scriptures. 3. Attending duly the public worship. 4. Partaking of the Sacrament. 5. Paying a due respect to God's ministers.

These might be all good things; but, as they were not the kind of good things that I expected from that text, I despaired of ever meeting with them from any other, was disgusted, and attended his preaching no more.

I had some years before composed a little Liturgy, or form of prayer, for my own private use (that is, in 1728), entitled, Articles of Belief and Acts of Religion. I returned to the use of this, and went no more to the public assemblies.

My conduct might be blamable, but I leave it, without attempting further to excuse it; my present purpose being to relate facts, and not to make apologies for them.

Notice that Franklin had, at twenty-two years of age, given considerable thought to religion, and had composed his own worship service. (A "liturgy" is a worship service.)

* * * * *

Church Structures

Here, Madison argues against any special privileges being given religious groups – in this case, the chartering of church corporations.

James Madison
Monopolies, Perpetuities, Corporations, Ecclesiastical Endowments, Date Uncertain
Besides the danger of a direct mixture of religion and civil government, there is an evil which ought to be guarded

against in the indefinite accumulation of property from the capacity of holding it in perpetuity by ecclesiastical corporations.

The establishment of the chaplainship in Congress is a palpable violation of equal rights as well as of Constitutional principles.

The danger of silent accumulations and encroachments by ecclesiastical bodies has not sufficiently engaged attention in the U.S.

∗ ∗ ∗ ∗ ∗

Coercion

Here, Washington and Madison argue that coercion is required. It is noteworthy that they were honest about the issue: Modern politicians in favor of coercion nearly always find clever ways to avoid admitting it.

It would have been interesting to hear how these two men divided between "coercion" and "tyranny," but, to my knowledge, no such clarification exists.

George Washington
Letter to John Jay, August 1, 1786
Experience has taught us that men will not adopt and carry into execution measures the best calculated for their own good without the intervention of a coercive power.

∗ ∗ ∗ ∗ ∗

James Madison
Notes on the Confederacy, April, 1787
A sanction is essential to the idea of law, as coercion is to that of Government.

∗ ∗ ∗ ∗ ∗

Commerce

George Washington
Letter to Benjamin Harrison October 10, 1784
A people... who are possessed of the spirit of commerce, who see and who will pursue their advantages may achieve almost anything.

* * * * *

Commerce & Taxes

It is interesting to notice Hamilton's reasons for favoring commerce over farming – that it is better for tax-gathering. (Washington, in the quote under "Commerce" praises it for other reasons.)

Alexander Hamilton
Federalist #12
The ability of a country to pay taxes must always be proportioned, in a great degree, to the quantity of money in circulation, and to the speed with which it circulates.

Commerce, contributing to both these objects, must of necessity render the payment of taxes easier, and facilitate the requisite supplies to the treasury.

The hereditary dominions of the Emperor of Germany contain a great extent of fertile, cultivated, and populous territory, a large proportion of which is situated in mild and luxuriant climates. In some parts of this territory are to be found the best gold and silver mines in Europe. And yet, from the want of the fostering influence of commerce, that monarch can boast but slender revenues. He has several times been compelled to owe obligations to the monetary assistance of other nations for the preservation of his essential interests, and is unable, upon the strength of his own resources, to sustain a long or continued war.

Note also Hamilton's clear understanding of economics, including concepts that we now call money supply and velocity.

* * * * *

Alexander Hamilton
Federalist #12
The pockets of the farmers, on the other hand, will reluctantly yield but scanty supplies, in the unwelcome shape of impositions on their houses and lands; and personal property is too precarious and invisible a fund to be laid hold of in any other way than by the imperceptible agency of taxes on consumption.

* * * * *

Compromise

This is Sam Adams' rejection of the Carlisle Peace Commission, which was a group of British negotiators who were sent, in 1778, with a belated offer of self-rule, within the British Empire.

Samuel Adams
Letter to the Earl of Carlisle, July 16, 1778
To revive mutual affection is utterly impossible. We freely forgive you, but it is not in nature that you should forgive us. You have injured us too much.

An insightful comment by Adams that the British would not be able to forgive the Americans – not because the Americans had done bad things, but because the British had. In order to justify one's aggressions, the target of those actions must be seen as deserving them… and if they are easy to forgive, one must question one's actions.

* * * * *

The Confidence of The People

George Washington
Letter to Joseph Reed, July 4, 1780
The best way to preserve the confidence of the people durably is to promote their true interests.

* * * * *

Congress

In this first quote, the astute Madison points out that men are more comfortable misbehaving in groups than they are individually:

James Madison
Letter to Thomas Jefferson, October 24, 1787
The conduct of every popular assembly... shows that individuals join without remorse in acts against which their consciences would revolt, if proposed to them, separately, in their closets.

* * * * *

Samuel Adams
Boston Gazette, December 9, 1771
Does it make any real difference whether one man has the sovereign disposal of the peoples purses, or five hundred?

In other words, that a legislature, by itself, provides no real safety.

* * * * *

Samuel Adams
Letter to James Warren December 26, 1775
Even public Bodies of men legally constituted are too prone to covet more power than the public hath judged it safe to entrust them with.

* * * * *

Samuel Adams
Letter to Elbridge Gerry January 2, 1776
I hope our country will never see the time, when either riches or the want of them will be the leading considerations in the choice of public officers.

Whenever riches shall be deemed a necessary qualification, ambition as well as avarice will prompt men most earnestly to thirst for them, and it will be commonly said, as in ancient times of degeneracy, "Get money, money still, and then let virtue follow if she will."

* * * * *

Thomas Jefferson
Letter to Francis W. Gilmer June 27, 1816
Our legislators are not sufficiently apprized of the rightful limits of their power; that their true office is to declare and enforce only our natural rights and duties, and to take none of them from us.

* * * * *

Conscription

Here Washington expresses his belief that since the military provides protection to all (regardless of property or lack thereof), every (male) citizen must contribute by serving in those armed forces.

George Washington
Letter to Alexander Hamilton May 2, 1783

It may be laid down, as a primary position, and the basis of our system, that every citizen who enjoys the protection of a free government, owes not only a proportion of his property, but even of his personal services to the defense of it, and consequently that the Citizens of America (with a few legal and official exceptions) from 18 to 50 Years of Age should be borne on the Militia Rolls, provided with uniform Arms, and so far accustomed to the use of them, that the Total strength of the Country might be called forth at Short Notice on any very interesting Emergency.

* * * * *

The Constitution & Liberty

Founders did not think of the Constitution as something that secured their liberty. Liberty, in their eyes, was always and only associated with the virtues of the American people, and did not descend from any set of documents and rules, even those of the Constitution.

Samuel Adams
Public Advertiser, 1749

Neither the wisest constitution nor the wisest laws will secure the liberty and happiness of a people whose manners are universally corrupt.

* * * * *

John Adams

Letter to Zabdiel Adams June 21, 1776

The only foundation of a free Constitution is pure Virtue, and if this cannot be inspired into our People in a greater Measure than they have it now, they may change their Rulers and the forms of Government, but they will not obtain a lasting Liberty. They will only exchange Tyrants and Tyrannies.

* * * * *

John Adams

Letter to the Officers of the First Brigade of the Third Division of the Militia of Massachusetts October 11, 1798

We have no government armed with power capable of contending with human passions unbridled by morality and religion. Avarice, ambition, revenge, or gallantry, would break the strongest cords of our Constitution as a whale goes through a net.

Our Constitution was made only for a religious and moral people. It is wholly inadequate for the government of any other.

* * * * *

The Constitution, Opinions Regarding

Samuel Adams

Letter to Richard Henry Lee December 3, 1787

Considering the new Constitution as it is already called... I confess, as I enter the building I stumble at the threshold. I meet with a National Government, instead of a Federal Union of Sovereign States. I am not able to conceive why the wisdom of the convention led them to give the preference to the former before the latter.

If the several states in the union are to become one entire Nation, under one legislature, the powers of which shall extend to every subject of legislation, and its laws be supreme

& control the whole, the idea of sovereignty in these States must be lost.

When Adams writes "several states" he means "separate states." The meaning of the word has changed over time.

* * * * *

Samuel Adams
Letter to Elbridge Gerry August 22, 1789
I hope Congress, before they adjourn, will take into very serious consideration the necessary Amendments of the Constitution.

Those whom I call the best—the most judicious & disinterested Federalists, who wish for the perpetual Union, Liberty & Happiness of the States & their respective Citizens, many of them if not all are anxiously expecting them.

They wish to see a Line drawn as clearly as may be, between the federal Powers vested in Congress and the distinct Sovereignty of the several States upon which the private & personal Rights of the Citizens depend. Without such distinction there will be danger of the Constitution developing imperceptibly and gradually into a consolidated Government over all the States.

* * * * *

George Washington
Letter to Patrick Henry, September 24, 1787
I wish the constitution, which is offered, had been made more perfect; but I sincerely believe it is the best that could be obtained at this time. And, as a constitutional door is opened for amendment hereafter, the adoption of it, under the present circumstances of the Union, is in my opinion desirable.

* * * * *

James Madison
Letter to Thomas Jefferson, March 19, 1787

I think myself that it will be expedient... to lay the foundation of the new system in such a ratification by the people themselves of the several States as will render it clearly paramount to their Legislative authorities.

* * * * *

Thomas Jefferson
Letter to John Taylor November 26, 1798

I wish it were possible to obtain a single amendment to our Constitution. I would be willing to depend on that alone for the reduction of the administration of our government to the genuine principles of its Constitution; I mean an additional article, taking from the federal government the power of borrowing.

* * * * *

George Washington
Farewell Address September 17, 1796

The basis of our political systems is the right of the people to make and to alter their Constitutions of Government. But the Constitution which at any time exists, till changed by an explicit and authentic act of the whole people, is sacredly obligatory upon all.

* * * * *

Benjamin Franklin
Speech to the Constitutional Convention June 28, 1787

I agree to this Constitution, with all its faults, — if they are such; because I think a general Government necessary for us, and there is no form of government but what may be a blessing to the people, if well administered; and I believe, farther, that this is likely to be well administered for a course of years, and can only end in despotism, as other forms have done before it, when the people shall become so corrupted as to need despotic government, being incapable of any other.

* * * * *

Alexander Hamilton
Statement after the Constitutional Convention 1787
For my own part, I sincerely esteem it a system which without the finger of God, never could have been suggested and agreed upon by such a diversity of interests.

* * * * *

Constitution, Design Of

James Madison
Letter to Thomas Jefferson, October 24, 1787
The great necessity in government is to modify the sovereignty, so that it may be sufficiently neutral between different parts of the society, to control one part from invading the rights of another, and at the same time sufficiently control itself from setting up an interest adverse to that of the entire society.

* * * * *

James Madison
Federalist #39
The proposed Constitution, therefore, is, in strictness, neither a national nor a federal Constitution, but a composition of both.

- In its foundation it is federal, not national;

- In the sources from which the ordinary powers of the government are drawn, it is partly federal and partly national;

- In the operation of these powers, it is national, not federal;

- In the extent of them, again, it is federal, not national; and, finally,

- In the authoritative mode of introducing amendments, it is neither wholly federal nor wholly national.

Here Madison, the architect of the Constitution, explains the structure of the government he designed. Note that Madison very specifically differentiates between "national" powers and "federal" powers.

"National" powers are those of an independent central government.

"Federal" powers are those that come from the contributions of the states. The meaning of "federal" was "a union based on a treaty." So, federal powers were ones that the states provided according to the (treaty-like) Constitution.

* * * * *

Alexander Hamilton
Federalist #78
The judiciary is beyond comparison the weakest of the three departments of power; that it can never attack with success either of the other two.

* * * * *

Alexander Hamilton
Federalist #78
The complete independence of the courts justice is peculiarly essential in a limited Constitution.

* * * * *

Constitution, Necessity Of

George Washington
Letter to John Jay August 15, 1786

If you tell the Legislatures they have violated the treaty of peace and invaded the prerogatives of the confederacy they will laugh in your face. What then is to be done?

Things cannot go on in the same train forever. It is much to be feared, as you observe, that the better kind of people being disgusted with the circumstances will have their minds prepared for any revolution whatever. We are apt to run from one extreme into another.

To anticipate & prevent disastrous contingencies would be the part of wisdom & patriotism. What astonishing changes a few years are capable of producing! I am told that even respectable characters speak of a monarchical form of government without horror. From thinking proceeds speaking, thence to acting is often but a single step. But how irrevocable & tremendous! What a triumph for the advocates of despotism to find that we are incapable of governing ourselves, and that systems founded on the basis of equal liberty are merely ideal & fallacious!

Would to God that wise measures may be taken in time to avert the consequences we have but too much reason to apprehend.

When Washington uses the word "tremendous" above, he is referring to size, not quality. "Huge" would be the modern equivalent.

* * * * *

Alexander Hamilton
Federalist #21

The United States, as now composed, have no powers to exact obedience, or punish disobedience to their resolutions.

* * * * *

The Constitutional Convention

George Washington
Constitutional Convention of 1787

Let us raise a standard to which the wise and honest can repair; the rest is in the hands of God.

* * * * *

James Madison
Letter to George Washington, April 16, 1787

To give the new system its proper validity and energy, a ratification must be obtained from the people, and not merely from the ordinary authority of the Legislatures.

* * * * *

The Corruption of The Republic

Many of the founders were deeply concerned with their government being corrupted. Following are some of their thoughts:

Samuel Adams
Letter to Richard Henry Lee August 29, 1789

I now most sincerely believe that while President Washington continues in the Chair he will be able to give to all good Men a satisfactory Reason for every Instance of his public Conduct...

Who will succeed the present President? For it is the lot of Man to die. Perhaps the next and the next may inherit his Virtues. But my Friend, I fear the Time will come, when a Bribe shall remove the most excellent Man from Office for the Purpose of making Room for the worst. It will be called an Error in Judgment. The Bribe will be concealed. It may however be vehemently suspected & who, in times of great degeneracy will venture to investigate and detect the corrupt practices of great Men?

Unless a sufficient Check is provided and clearly ascertained for every Power given, will not the Constitution and the Liberties of the Citizens… finally be subverted?

* * * * *

Samuel Adams

Boston Gazette, April 2, 1781

Those who are to have a Share in making as well as in judging and executing the Laws should be Men of singular Wisdom and Integrity. Such as are conscious that they are deficient in either of these Qualities, should even Tremble at being named as Candidates!

I hope the great Business of Elections will never be left by the many, to be done by the few; for before we are aware of it, that few may become the Engine of Corruption--the Tool of a Junta.—Heaven forbid!

* * * * *

Here Adams says that men opposed to American liberties have had seats in congress from the beginning of the Continental Congress in 1774. It concerns him that such men are still in Congress (the Revolutionary War still underway at this time) and that they will be in Congress in the future.

Samuel Adams

Letter to Richard Henry Lee January 15, 1781

Let us recur to first Principles without Delay.

It is our Duty, to make every proper exertion in our respective States to revive the old patriotic feelings among the People at large, and to get the public Departments, especially the most important of them, filled with Men of Understanding & inflexible Virtue.

It would be indeed alarming, if the United States should ever entrust the Ship in which our all is at Stake, with inexperienced or unprincipled Pilots. Our Cause is surely too interesting to Mankind, to be put under the Direction of Men, vain, avaricious or concealed under the Hypocritical Guise of Patriotism, without a Spark of public or private Virtue. We may possibly be more in Danger of this, than many of our honest Citizens may imagine.

Is there not Reason to think that even those who are opposed to our Cause may steal into Places of the highest Trust? I need not remind you that Men of this Character have had Seats in Congress from the beginning...

If it was so in those Times of Vigilance & Zeal, how much more is it to be expected, when the Love of many has grown cold, & their Minds are distracted with the Pursuit of Pleasure & exorbitant Riches.

We cannot be persuaded to believe that bad Men have been sent by their States with a View of giving a fatal Stab to our Cause in its Infancy; but is it unreasonable to suppose that their Elections were secretly influenced by artful Men, with that Design. Our most dangerous Enemies may be in our Bosoms.

* * * * *

Thomas Jefferson
Letter to Nathaniel Macon, 1821
Our government is now taking so steady a course as to show by what road it will pass to destruction. That is: by consolidation first, and then corruption, its necessary consequence.

* * * * *

Thomas Jefferson
Letter to William T. Berry, 1822
If ever this vast country is brought under a single government, it will be one of the most extensive corruption, indifferent and incapable of a wholesome care over so wide a spread of surface.

Courage & Cowardice

It is one thing to read and hear about rebellion and fighting for liberty, but it is quite another to do it. Courage is required, and it is required at times when avoiding it is far easier.

Samuel Adams
Boston Gazette February 3, 1776

"But," say the puling, pusillanimous cowards, "we shall be subject to a long and bloody war, if we declare independence." On the contrary, I affirm it the only step that can bring the contest to a speedy and happy issue. By declaring independence we put ourselves on a footing for an equal negotiation. Now we are called a pack of villainous rebels, who, like the St. Vincent's Indians, can expect nothing more than a pardon for our lives, and the sovereign favor respecting freedom, and property to be at the King's will. Grant, Almighty God, that I may be numbered with the dead before that sable day dawns on North America.

"Pusillanimous" means "lacking in courage or resolution."

* * * * *

Samuel Adams
Speech in Philadelphia August 1, 1776

If ye love wealth better than liberty, the tranquility of servitude than the animated contest of freedom — go home from us in peace. We ask not your counsels or arms. Crouch down and lick the hands which feed you. May your chains sit lightly upon you, and may posterity forget that you were our countrymen!

* * * * *

By 1770 it was clear that the minds of the American colonists had taken in John Locke's idea of Natural Rights, that they had reconciled them with their Christian beliefs, and that the rule of the King from three thousand miles away was not going to be compatible with their new mentality. At that moment, the town meeting of Boston chose Adams to serve in their cause. Adams, knowing it was the right thing to do, accepted, but then had to face the consequences. We can imagine him walking home, contemplating what he was going to tell his wife: He was destined to stand up to the King of England and defy him. Being chased and imprisoned was likely, death was a distinct possibility. And he had to go home and tell his wife about it. Here is his account of that night:

John Adams
Letter to Benjamin Rush April 12, 1809
When I went home to my family in May, 1770, from the town meeting in Boston, which was the first I had ever attended, and where I had been chosen in my absence, without any solicitation, one of their representatives, I said to my wife, "I have accepted a seat in the House of Representatives, and thereby have consented to my own ruin, to your ruin, and to the ruin of our children. I give you this warning, that you may prepare your mind for your fate." She burst into tears, but instantly cried out in a transport of magnanimity, "Well, I am willing in this cause to run all risks with you, and be ruined with you, if you are ruined." These were times, my friend, in Boston, which tried women's souls as well as men's.

"Trying their souls" is a very fair characterization of such events. It sounds romantic in a novel – it isn't in real life. Adams was most fortunate that his wife, Abigail, passed that test.

* * * * *

Benjamin Franklin
Notes February 1775
They who can give up essential liberty to obtain a little temporary safety, deserve neither liberty nor safety.

* * * * *

Criticism

Samuel Adams
Letter to John Hancock May 11 1770)

You say you have been spoken ill of. What then? Can you think that while you are a good Man that all will speak well of you?

If you knew the person who has defamed you, nothing is more likely than that you would justly value yourself upon that man's Censure as being the highest Applause.

Those who were fond of continuing Mr. Otis on the Seat, were I dare say to a Man among your warmest friends: Will you then add to their Disappointment by a Resignation, merely because one contemptible person, who perhaps was hired for the purpose, has blessed you with his reviling?

Need I add more than to entreat it as a favor that you would alter your design. I am with strict truth Your affectionate friend & Brother.

* * * * *

Thomas Jefferson
Letter to Edward Dowse April 19, 1803

There is no act, however virtuous, for which ingenuity may not find some bad motive.

* * * * *

Jefferson reveals his sensitive nature:

Thomas Jefferson
Letter to F. Hopkinson March 13, 1789

I find the pain of a little censure, even when it is unfounded, is more acute than the pleasure of much praise.

* * * * *

The Current of Passions

Washington gives his advice, which he does not think powerful enough to stand against the current of men's passions. He expects this current of passions to eventually ruin the nation, as it has so many others.

George Washington
Farewell Address September 17, 1796
In offering to you, my countrymen, these counsels of an old and affectionate friend, I dare not hope they will make the strong and lasting impression I could wish; that they will control the usual current of the passions, or prevent our nation from running the course, which has hitherto marked the destiny of nations.

* * * * *

Danger & Distress

As mentioned above in the section entitled "Courage & Cowardice," reading about rebellion is a far cry from undertaking it. Here are the writings of Samuel Adams to his wife, Betsy, in the middle of the great struggle. This is courage in action.

Samuel Adams
Letter to his wife December 11, 1776
If this City should be surrendered, I will by no means despair of our Cause. It is a righteous Cause and I am fully persuaded righteous Heaven will succeed it.

Congress will adjourn to Baltimore in Maryland, about 120 Miles from this place, when Necessity requires it and not before.

It is agreed to appoint a Day of Prayer, & a Committee will bring in a Resolution for that purpose this day. I wish we were a more religious People.

* * * * *

Here we see Sam Adams, going through his days knowing that threats confront his entire family. He hasn't received letters from her, he worries that she is sick, he thinks she is on the run, but he's not sure where.

Samuel Adams
Letter to his wife during the early days of the war June 16, 1775
MY DEAR,

I have so often wrote to you, without having a single Line in Answer to one of my Letters, that I have doubted whether you have received any of them.

Had I not heard that you dined with some of my Friends at Cambridge about a fortnight [two weeks] ago I should have suspected that you had changed your Place of Abode at Dedham and that therefore my Letters had not reached you, or I should have been very anxious lest by some bodily Indisposition you were rendered unable to write to me.

It is painful to me to be absent from you.

As your Letters would in some Measure afford me Relief, I beg you would omit no Opportunity of writing. Your Backwardness leads me to conclude that something has happened which would be disagreeable to me to hear. If any ill Accident has befallen my Son or any other person dear to me, I would choose to hear it.

Our Boston Friends are – some of them – confined in a Garrison [fort], others dispersed, I know not where. Pray, my dear, let me know as much about them as you can.

I make no Doubt but it will be a pleasure to you to hear that I am in good Health and Spirits.

I wish I could consistently inform you what is doing here. I can however tell you that Matters go on, though slower than one could wish, yet agreeable to my Mind.

My Love to all Friends. I earnestly recommend you and them to the Protection and Blessing of Heaven. The Bearer is waiting for this Letter, I must therefore conclude with assuring you that I am with the greatest Sincerity, my dear Betsy,

Your affectionate husband and Friend

Note that Adams asks her to please tell him if their son or their friends have been captured or dead, saying "I would choose to hear it." And when he says, "I wish I could consistently inform you what is doing here," he means that he can't risk putting such sensitive information into a letter, lest it be captured by the British and lead to disaster.

* * * * *

Samuel Adams
Letter to his wife during the early days of the war June 17, 1775
We have had Occasion to detain the Bearer which gives me the Pleasure of acknowledging your very acceptable and obliging Letter of the 6th instantly. I am rejoiced to hear that you are recovered from a late Indisposition of Body. I pray God to confirm your Health.

I wonder that you have received but one Letter from me since I left Worcester. I wrote to you at Hartford and New York and I do not know how often since I came into this City.

It is a great Satisfaction to me to be assured from you that your Mother & Family are out of Boston, and also my boy Job. I commend him for his Contrivance in getting out. Tell him from me to be a good Boy.

I wish to hear that my Son and honest Surry were released from their Confinement in that Town. I am much pleased my dear with the good Sense and public Spirit you discovered in your Answer to Major Kain's Message.

Your Concern for my comfortable Subsistence here is very kind and obliging to me. When I am in need of money I will write to you.

* * * * *

Samuel Adams

Letter to his wife during the early days of the war June 28, 1775
MY DEAR BETSY,

Yesterday I received Letters from some of our Friends at the Camp informing me of the Engagement between the American Troops and the Rebel Army, in Charlestown. I cannot but be greatly rejoiced at the tried Valor of our Countrymen, who by all Accounts behaved with an intrepidity becoming those who fought for their Liberties against the mercenary Soldiers of a Tyrant.

It is painful to me to reflect upon the Terror I must suppose you were under on hearing the Noise of War so near you. Favor me, my dear, with an Account of your Apprehensions at that time, under your own hand.

I pray God to cover the heads of our Countrymen in every day of Battle, and ever to protect you from Injury in these distracted Times.

The Death of our truly amiable and worthy Friend Dr Warren is greatly afflicting. The Language of Friendship is, how shall we resign him! But it is our Duty to submit to the Dispensations of Heaven, "Whose Ways are ever gracious, ever just." He fell in the glorious Struggle for the public Liberty.

Mr. Pitts and Dr Church inform me that my dear Son has at length escaped from the Prison of Boston. I have enclosed a letter to him, which I desire you would seal and deliver to him, or send it to him if he is not with you.

Remember me to my dear Hannah and Sister Polly and to all Friends. Let me know where good old Surry is.

Gage has made me respectable by naming me first among those who are to receive no favor from him. I thoroughly despise him and his Proclamation. It is the Subject of Ridicule here, as you may see by the enclosed which I have taken from this day's paper.

I am in good health and Spirits. Pray my dear let me have your Letters more frequently--by every opportunity.

The Clock is now striking twelve. I therefore wish you a good
Night.

*His son imprisoned and escaped, a dear friend killed, deep concerns for other family
members and friends. Through it all, the Adams' endure and continue... as indeed
they did for years to follow.*

*When Adams refers to Gage making him "respectable," he is using sarcasm.
General Gage, Governor of Massachusetts, had offered pardons to people involved in
the battles of Lexington & Concord, except to Samuel Adams and John Hancock.*

* * * * *

Death

*As much as any other people, the founders dealt with death. Following are their
thoughts regarding death and dying.*

*In this first quote, Jefferson writes to Abigail Adams, in the last year of her life, at
about 73 years of age. She is approaching death, knows it, and is corresponding
with the aged, wise Jefferson, a friend since youth.*

Thomas Jefferson
Letter to Mrs. John (Abigail) Adams 1817
Our next meeting must be in the country to which [the years]
have flown—a country for us not now very distant. For this
journey we shall need neither gold nor silver in our purse, nor
scrip nor coats nor staves. Nor is the provision for it more
easy than the preparation has been kind. Nothing proves
more than this, that the Being who presides over the world is
essentially benevolent. Stealing from us one by one the
faculties of enjoyment, searing our sensibilities, leading us like
the horse in his mill, round and round the same beaten circle,
. . until, satiated and fatigued with this leaden iteration, we ask
our own leave.

I heard once a very old friend, who had troubled himself with
neither poets nor philosophers, say the same thing in plain

prose, that he was tired of pulling off his shoes and stockings at night, and putting them on again in the morning.

The "country" Jefferson refers to is the afterlife, and by saying "not now distant," he refers to the fact that they are both old and approaching death rather sooner than later. "Neither gold nor silver" is a reference to Matthew 10:9.

* * * * *

Thomas Jefferson
Letter to John Adams April, 1816
You ask if I would agree to live my seventy, or rather seventy-three, years over again? To which I say yes. I think, with you, that it is a good world on the whole – that it has been framed on a principle of benevolence, and more pleasure than pain dealt out to us.

There are indeed (those who might say no) gloomy and hypochondriac minds, inhabitants of diseased bodies, disgusted with the present and despairing of the future, always counting the worst will happen because it may happen.

To these I say, How much pain have the evils which never happened cost us!

My temperament is optimistic...

* * * * *

Thomas Jefferson
Letter to M. Correa, 1817
[Death] the great problem, untried by the living, unreported by the dead.

On the night before Jefferson's death - the third of July - he sat up in bed, went through the motions of writing, and said some partly intelligible words about the Revolutionary Committee of Safety, which were the earliest origins of self-government in America, beginning in the 1760s. As he lay approaching death, he asked once or twice if it was the fourth, and when told at last that it was, he was satisfied. He died at one o'clock in the afternoon, about five hours before his old friend John Adams.

After his death, his daughter Martha opened a paper that he had given her two days prior. It spoke of his loving thankfulness for her devotion to him, saying that parting from her was "the last pang of life," and promising to bear her love to the "two seraphs," her mother and her little sister, long dead, who now awaited him.

* * * * *

George Washington
Letter to Burwell Bassett, on the death of his stepdaughter Patsy, June 20, 1773

It is an easier matter to conceive, than to describe the distress of this Family; especially that of the unhappy Parent of our Dear Patsy Custis, when I inform you that two days ago the sweet Innocent Girl Entered into a more happy and peaceful abode than any she has met with in the afflicted Path she hitherto has trod.

* * * * *

Benjamin Franklin
Letter to George Whitefield, July 2, 1756

Life, like a dramatic piece, should... finish handsomely. Being now in the last act, I began to look for something fit to end with...

I settle a colony on the Ohio... to settle in that fine country a strong body of religious and industrious people!...

Might it not greatly facilitate the introduction of pure religion among the heathen, if we could, by such a colony, show them a better sample of Christians than they commonly see in our Indian traders?

* * * * *

Benjamin Franklin
His self-written Epitaph, April 17, 1790

THE BODY of BENJAMIN FRANKLIN Printer, Like the cover of an old book, Its contents torn out, And stripped of its lettering and gilding Lies here, food for worms; Yet the work itself shall not be lost, For it will (as he believed) appear once more, In a new, And more beautiful edition, Corrected and amended By the AUTHOR

* * * * *

Thomas Jefferson
Letter to John Adams November 13, 1818) (regarding the death of Adams' wife Abigail)

Tried myself in the school of affliction, by the loss of every form of connection which can rive the human heart, I know well, and feel what you have lost, what you have suffered, are suffering, and have yet to endure.

The same trials have taught me that for ills so immeasurable, time and silence are the only medicines. I will not, therefore, by useless condolences, open afresh the gates of your grief, nor, although mingling sincerely my tears with yours, will I say a word more where words are vain.

* * * * *

Benjamin Franklin
His parents' epitath

JOSIAH FRANKLIN,
and
ABIAH his Wife,
lie here interred.
They lived lovingly together in wedlock
fifty-five years.
Without an estate, or any gainful employment,
By constant labor and industry,
with God's blessing,
They maintained a large family
comfortably,
and brought up thirteen children
and seven grandchildren
reputably.
From this instance, reader,
Be encouraged to diligence in thy calling,

And distrust not Providence.
He was a pious and prudent man;
She, a discreet and virtuous woman.
Their youngest son,
In filial regard to their memory,
Places this stone.

* * * * *

Death and Taxes

Benjamin Franklin
Letter to Jean-Baptiste Leroy November 13, 1789
Our new Constitution is now established, and has an appearance that promises permanency; but in this world nothing can be said to be certain, except death and taxes.

* * * * *

The Declaration of Independence

Samuel Adams
Letter to Benjamin Kent July 27, 1776
It has been difficult for a Number of persons sent from all parts of so extensive a Territory and representing Colonies (or as I must now call them States) which in many Respects have had different Interests & Views, to unite in Measures materially to affect them all. Hence our Determinations have been necessarily slow.

We have however gone on from Step to Step, till at length we are arrived to perfection, as you have heard, in a Declaration of Independence.

Was there ever a Revolution brought about, especially so important as this, without great internal Tumults & violent Convulsions! The Delegates of every Colony in Congress have given their Voices in favor of the great Question, & the

People I am told, recognize the Resolution as though it were a Decree promulgated from Heaven.

I have thought that if this decisive measure had been taken six months earlier, it would have given Vigor to our Northern Army & a different Issue to our military Exertions in Canada. But probably I was mistaken. The Colonies were not then all ripe for so momentous a Change. It was necessary that they should be united, & it required Time & patience to remove old prejudices, to instruct the unenlightened, convince the doubting and fortify the timid.

* * * * *

John Adams
Letter to his wife July 3, 1776
Yesterday the greatest question was decided which ever was debated in America; and a greater perhaps never was, nor will be, decided among men.

A resolution was passed without one dissenting colony, "that these United Colonies are, and of right ought to be, free and independent States." ...

I am well aware of the Toil and Blood and Treasure, that it will cost Us to maintain this Declaration, and support and defend these States. Yet through all the Gloom I can see the Rays of ravishing Light and Glory. I can see that the End is more than worth all the Means.

And that Posterity will triumph in that Days Transaction, even although we should rue it, which I trust in God We shall not.

* * * * *

Alexander Hamilton
Federalist #84
The only use of the declaration was to recognize the ancient law and to remove doubts which might have been occasioned by the Revolution. This consequently can be considered as no part of a declaration of rights, which under our constitutions

must be intended as limitations of the power of the government itself.

* * * * *

Defending Liberty

Samuel Adams
Letter to Josiah Stone April 13 1773
May He who gave this land to our worthy forefathers, animate us their posterity to defend it at all Hazards; and while we would not lose the Character of loyal subjects to a prince resolved to protect us, we will yet never forfeit that of Men determined to be free.

* * * * *

Deism

Franklin describes how he came to consider himself a deist.

Benjamin Franklin
Autobiography 1787
My parents had early given me religious impressions, and brought me through my childhood piously in the Dissenting way. But I was scarce fifteen, when, after doubting by turns of several points, as I found them disputed in the different books I read, I began to doubt of Revelation itself.

Some books against Deism fell into my hands; they were said to be the substance of sermons preached at Boyle's Lectures. It happened that they wrought an effect on me quite contrary to what was intended by them; for the arguments of the Deists, which were quoted to be refuted, appeared to me much stronger than the refutations; in short, I soon became a thorough Deist.

The Dissenters were non-conformist Christians.

* * * * *

Franklin describes the beliefs that he considers deistic.

Benjamin Franklin
His Autobiography, 1774
I never doubted, for instance, the existence of the Deity; that he made the world, and governed it by his Providence; that the most acceptable service of God was the doing good to man; that our souls are immortal; and that all crime will be punished, and virtue rewarded, either here or hereafter.

These I esteemed the essentials of every religion; and, being to be found in all the religions we had in our country, I respected them all, though with different degrees of respect, as I found them more or less mixed with other articles, which, without any tendency to inspire, promote, or confirm morality, served principally to divide us, and make us unfriendly to one another.

This respect to all, with an opinion that even the worst had some good effects, induced me to avoid all discussions that might tend to lessen the good opinion another might have of his own religion; and as our province increased in people, and new places of worship were continually wanted, and generally erected by voluntary contributions, my contribution for such purposes, whatever might be the sect, was never refused.

* * * * *

Desperation

George Washington
After the fall of Fort Washington, 1776
If I were to put a curse on my worst enemy, it would to be to wish him in my position now. I just do not know what to do.

It seems impossible to continue my command in this situation, but if I withdraw, all will be lost.

* * * * *

Difficulties

Thomas Jefferson
Letter to Lafayette April 2, 1790
We are not to expect to be translated from despotism to liberty in a featherbed.

* * * * *

Thomas Jefferson
Letter to Archibald Stuart December 23, 1791
I would rather be exposed to the inconveniences attending too much liberty, than those attending too small a degree of it.

* * * * *

George Mason
Letter to George Washington (April 5, 1769)
Our All is at stake, and the little conveniences and comforts of Life, compared to our Liberty, ought to be rejected, not with reluctance but with Pleasure.

* * * * *

Disappointment

Samuel Adams
Letter to Samuel Cooper April 30, 1776
I am disappointed but I bear it tolerably well.

* * * * *

Disobedience To Armed Officials

It should be remembered that the revolutionaries began as individuals defying armed officials of the most respected and democratic government on Earth.

Samuel Adams
Boston Gazette, December 10, 1770

I declare my opinion, that a cause of so great importance, not only to this town, but to all his Majesty's subjects, and especially to the inhabitants of cities and sea-port towns: They are exposed to have troops posted among them, whenever the present administration shall take it into their heads in his Majesty's name to send them.

Such a cause ought to be fairly stated to the public, that we may determine how far we are bound to submit to every band of soldiers we may meet in the streets, and in what instances we may venture to stand against them and prevent them from murdering those whom we may think to be innocent persons, without being liable to be censured for acting unlawfully – if we escape with our own heads after falling victims to their rage and cruelty.

* * * * *

Duty To Posterity

Samuel Adams
Letter James Warren December 25, 1776

How necessary is it then for our Countrymen to strain every Nerve to defeat their Design. The Time is short. Let this be the only Subject of our Thoughts and Consultation. Our Affairs in France wear a promising Aspect. Let us do our Duty and defend the fair Inheritance which our Fathers have left us—our pious Forefathers who regarded Posterity & fought and bled that they might transmit to us the Blessing of Liberty.

Samuel Adams

Letter to Horatio Gates May 2 1783

I most heartily congratulate you on the Return of Peace with Liberty & Independence.--Blessings for which Patriots have toiled & Heroes fought & bled. Our Country may now be happy if she is not wanting to her self.

We have done our Duty. Future Generations can never curse the present for carelessly surrendering their Rights.

* * * * *

Samuel Adams

Letter to his wife January 29, 1777

I am now more convinced of any thing than that it is my Duty, to oppose to the utmost of my Ability the Designs of those who would enslave my Country; and with God's Assistance I am resolved to oppose them till their Designs are defeated or I am called to quit the Stage of Life.

* * * * *

Samuel Adams

Letter to Richard Henry Lee December 23, 1784

Better it would have been for us to have fallen in our highly famed Struggle for our Rights, or even to have remained in our ignoble State of Bondage hoping for better Times, than now to become a contemptible Nation.

The World has given us an exalted Character, & thus have laid on us a heavy Tax!

* * * * *

Each Other

Samuel Adams
Letter to Arthur Lee May 17, 1773
You cannot write me too often.

* * * * *

Samuel Adams
Letter to Richard Henry Lee April 10, 1773
I had frequently heard of your Character and Merit, as a warm Advocate for Virtue and Liberty.

* * * * *

Samuel Adams
Letter to his wife February 1, 1781
James Rivington has published in his Royal Gazette, that the Acrimony between Mr. Hancock & me, was owing to his Attachment to General Washington, & my being on the Contrary, desirous of his Removal. This is an old Story which Men have believed and disbelieved as they pleased, without much Concern of mine.

It was a pitiful Contrivance to render me obnoxious to the General & our common Friends. If there has been any Difference between Mr. H and me, Rivington knows not the Origin of it. Mr. Hancock never thought me an Enemy to Gen1 Washington. He never thought that I was desirous of his being removed, & therefore could never treat me with Acrimony on that Account. I never wished for the Removal of General Washington, but if I had even attempted to effect it, it might have been an Evidence of my Deficiency in Judgment, or Rashness, but it could be no Evidence that I was his Enemy.

* * * * *

Thomas Jefferson
Letter to Samuel Adams, 1801

I addressed a letter to you, my very dear and ancient friend, on the 4th of March; not indeed to you by name, but through the medium of some of my fellow citizens, whom occasion called on me to address.

In meditating the matter of that address, I often asked myself, is this exactly in the spirit of the patriarch of liberty, Samuel Adams? Is it as he would express it? Will he approve of it? I have felt a great deal for our country in the times we have seen. But, individually, for no one so much as yourself.

When I have been told that you were avoided, insulted, frowned on, I could not but ejaculate, "Father, forgive them, for they know what they do." I confess I felt an indignation for you, which for myself I have been able, under every trial, to keep entirely passive.

How much I lament that time has deprived me of your aid. It would have been a day of glory which should have called you to the first office of the Administration. But give us your counsel and give us your blessing, and be assured that there exists not in the heart of man a more faithful esteem than mine to you.

* * * * *

John Adams prefers to be home with his wife and family, but he also appreciates that his fellow revolutionaries are "sages and heroes."

John Adams
Letter to his wife March 16, 1777

I long for rural and domestic scenes, for the warbling of Birds and the Prattle of my Children. Don't you think I am somewhat poetical this morning, for one of my Years, and considering the Gravity, and Insipidity of my Employment? — As much as I converse with Sages and Heroes, they have very little of my Love or Admiration. I should prefer the Delights of a Garden to the Dominion of a World.

John Adams
Last words, July 4, 1826
Thomas — Jefferson — still surv —

* * * * *

Thomas Jefferson
Letter to John Adams, 1825
You and I know that he [Richard Henry Lee] merited much during the Revolution. Eloquent, bold, and ever watchful at his post.

* * * * *

Thomas Jefferson
Autobiography, 1821
When the famous resolutions of 1765, against the Stamp Act, were proposed, I was yet a student of law in Williamsburg. I attended the debate, however, at the door of the lobby of the House of Burgesses and heard the splendid display of Mr. [Patrick] Henry's talents as a popular orator. They were great, indeed; such as I have never heard from any other man. He appeared to me to speak as Homer wrote.

* * * * *

Education

While the founders were strongly in favor of education, this is not to be confused with a modern "educational system." By "education," they meant people absorbing, understanding and learning how to use information, resulting in wisdom and virtue. They were not concerned with systems, rules or "social" matters — they wanted knowledge, wisdom and virtue and were more or less agnostic as to how that might be best accomplished.

Thomas Jefferson
Letter to Peter Carr August 10, 1787
State a moral case to a ploughman and a professor. The former will decide it as well, and often better than the latter, because he has not been led astray by artificial rules.

* * * * *

Thomas Jefferson
Notes on Religion October 1776
Truth.. seldom has received much aid from the power of great men to whom she is rarely known & seldom welcome.

* * * * *

Thomas Jefferson
Letter to John Tyler, 1810
I have two great measures at heart, without which no republic can maintain itself in strength.

1. That of general education, to enable every man to judge for himself what will secure or endanger his freedom.

2. To divide every county into hundreds, of such size that all the children of each will be within reach of a central school in it. But this division looks to many other fundamental provisions. Every hundred, besides a school, should have a justice of the peace, a constable, and a captain of militia...

* * * * *

George Washington
Letter to George Chapman, December 15, 1784

The best means of forming a manly, virtuous, and happy people will be found in the right education of youth. Without this foundation, every other means, in my opinion, must fail.

* * * * *

Samuel Adams
Letter to James Warren November 4, 1775

No people will tamely surrender their Liberties, nor can any be easily subdued, when knowledge is diffused and Virtue is preserved.

On the Contrary, when People are universally ignorant, and corrupted in their Manners, they will sink under their own weight without the Aid of foreign Invaders.

* * * * *

John Adams
Thoughts on Government, 1776

Laws for the liberal education of the youth, especially of the lower class of the people, are so extremely wise and useful, that, to a humane and generous mind, no expense for this purpose would be thought extravagant.

* * * * *

John Adams
Defense of the Constitutions 1787

Children should be educated and instructed in the principles of freedom.

* * * * *

Thomas Jefferson
Letter to Edward Barrington January 16, 1787
Cherish, therefore, the spirit of our people, and keep alive their attention. Do not be too severe upon their errors, but reclaim them by enlightening them.

* * * * *

Thomas Jefferson
Letter to John Page July 15, 1763
The most fortunate of us, in our journey through life, frequently meet with calamities and misfortunes which may greatly afflict us; and, to fortify our minds against the attacks of these calamities and misfortunes, should be one of the principal studies and endeavors of our lives.

* * * * *

Benjamin Franklin
Poor Richard's Almanac
A learned blockhead is a greater blockhead than an ignorant one.

* * * * *

The Election of 1800

The election of 1800 was bitter; full of lies and dirty tricks. After the election, Jefferson reversed many of the policies put in place during the preceding Presidency of John Adams. Hamilton fought desperately against Jefferson.

Alexander Hamilton
During the 1800 Election
If Mr. Pinckney [Jefferson's opponent] is not elected, a revolution will be the consequence, and within four years I will lose my head or be the leader of a triumphant army.

As it turned out, Jefferson became President and there were no plots against Hamilton. However, Hamilton continued to attack Vice President Aaron Burr in the newspapers, and the conflict led to a duel with firearms in 1804, in which Hamilton was killed.

* * * * *

Enemies

Samuel Adams
Letter to his wife October 20, 1778
Boston Friends tell me with great concern that I have Enemies there. I thank them for their concern for me, and tell them I knew it before.

The Man who acts an honest part in public life, must often counteract the Passions and Inclinations of weak and wicked Men, and this must create enemies.

I am therefore not disappointed or mortified. I flatter my self that no virtuous Man who knows me will or can be my Enemy; because I think he can have no Suspicion of my Integrity.

But they say my Enemies "are plotting against me." Neither does this discompose me, for what else can I expect from such Men. If they mean to make me uneasy they miss their Aim; for I am happy and it is not in their Power to disturb my Peace.

* * * * *

George Washington
Letter to John Banister, April 21, 1778
The most certain way to make a man your enemy is to tell him you esteem him such.

* * * * *

Equality

Samuel Adams

Boston Gazette, Dec. 11, 1770

But the constitution is a vain phantom, and the best laws are useless, if they are not religiously observed. The nation ought then to watch, and the true patriot will watch very attentively, in order to render them equally respected, by those who govern, and the people destined to obey.

* * * * *

Example

George Washington

Letter to Lord Stirling March 5, 1780

Example, whether it be good or bad, has a powerful influence.

* * * * *

Facts, Truth

George Washington

Letter to Major General Nathaniel Greene, January 22, 1780

Facts may speak for themselves.

* * * * *

John Adams

In Defense of the British Soldiers in the Boston Massacre Trials December 4, 1770

Facts are stubborn things; and whatever may be our wishes, our inclinations, or the dictates of our passion, they cannot alter the state of facts and evidence.

Note that Adams was defending British soldiers.

* * * * *

Faith

Benjamin Franklin
Poor Richard's Almanac July 1758
The Way to see by Faith, is to shut the Eye of Reason: The Morning Daylight appears plainer when you put out your Candle.

* * * * *

Family Status

Sam Adams is commenting here on a hereditary society that Alexander Hamilton founded immediately upon the end of the Revolutionary War – the Society of The Cincinnati. It was to be composed only of soldiers from the war, with membership restricted to their sons.

Samuel Adams
Letter to Elbridge Gerry April 19 1784
It appears wonderful that they could imagine a People who had freely spent their Blood & Treasure in Support of their equal rights & Liberties, could so soon be reconciled to the odious hereditary Distinction of Families.

This Country must be humiliated & debased to a great Degree, before they will patiently bear to see Individuals stalking with their assumed honorary Badges, & proudly boasting "These are the Distinctions of our Blood"

I cannot think that many of our Officers entertained such an Idea of haughty Pre-eminence; but the human Mind is so captivated with the Thought of being elevated above the ignoble Vulgar, that their Sons, if they should not themselves, when they perceive the Multitude grown giddy with gazing, may assume more than the mere Pageantry of Nobility.

When Men begin to applaud themselves, they are not easily persuaded to believe they can take a greater Share of Honor than justly belongs to them. They will be pleased with the Adulatory Addresses of other Men & flatter themselves that they are entitled to Power and Authority as well as the ostentatious Show of Superiority above their Equals.

I confess I greatly dislike the order. With you I think it dangerous & look upon it with the Eye of Jealousy. When the Pride of Family possesses the Minds of Men it is threatening to the Community in Proportion to the Good they have done. The unsuspecting People, when they are in a Mood to be grateful, will cry up the Virtues of their Benefactors & be ready to say, "Surely those Men who have done such great things for us, will never think of setting up a Tyranny over us."

Even Patriots & Heroes may become different Men when new & different Prospects shall have altered their Feelings & Views; and the undiscerning People may too late repent that they have suffered them to exalt themselves & their Family upon the Ruins of the Common Liberty.

* * * * *

Samuel Adams
Letter to Elbridge Gerry April 23, 1784
Cincinnati in Congress assembled are to meet at Philadelphia on the 5th of May & that General Washington is to preside.

That Gentleman has an idea of the Nature & Tendency of the Order very different from mine, otherwise I am certain he would never have given it his Sanction.

I look upon it to be as rapid a Stride towards an hereditary Military Nobility as was ever made in so short a Time. My Fears may be ill grounded, but if they are not, it is impossible for me not to think it a very great Misfortune to these States that he is a Member; for the Reputation he has justly acquired by his Conduct while Commander in Chief of our Armies, and the Gratitude & warm Affection which his Countrymen do & ought to feel towards him will give Weight to any thing he patronizes, & Luster to all who may be connected with him.

* * * * *

Samuel Adams
Letter to Richard Henry Lee December 3, 1787
You are sensible, Sir, that the Seeds of Aristocracy began to spring even before the Conclusion of our Struggle for the natural Rights of Men, Seeds which like a Canker Worm lie at the Root of free Governments. So great is the Wickedness of some Men, & the stupid Servility of others, that one would be almost inclined to conclude that Communities cannot be free.

The few haughty Families, think they must govern. The Body of the People tamely consent & submit to be their Slaves. This unravels the Mystery of Millions being enslaved by the few!

* * * * *

Fear Of Change

Samuel Adams describes how the defenders of liberty were portrayed as wild and dangerous men. The goal of these portrayals was to upset the lazy and to turn them against the revolutionaries, as people who would complicate their lives and upset things.

Samuel Adams
Boston Gazette, December 9, 1771
If the liberties of America are ever completely ruined, of which in my opinion there is now the utmost danger, it will in all probability be the consequence of a mistaken notion of prudence, which leads men to acquiesce in measures of the most destructive tendency for the sake of present ease.

When designs are formed to raze the very foundation of a free government, those few who are to erect their grandeur and fortunes upon the general ruin, will employ every art to sooth the devoted people into a state of indolence, inattention and security, which is forever the fore-runner of slavery.

They are alarmed at nothing so much, as attempts to awaken the people to jealousy and watchfulness; and it has been an old game played over and over again, to hold up the men who would rouse their fellow citizens and countrymen to a sense of their real danger, and inspire them to the most zealous activity in the use of all proper means for the preservation of the public liberty, as "pretended patriots," "intemperate politicians," rash, hot-headed men, Incendiaries, wretched desperadoes, who, as was said of the best of men, would turn the world upside down, or have done it already.

"Turn the world upside down" is a reference to Acts 17:6 and the early missionary journey of Paul and Silas.

* * * * *

Fines, Punishments

George Mason
Virginia Declaration of Rights 1776
That excessive bail ought not to be required, nor excessive fines imposed; nor cruel and unusual punishments inflicted.

* * * * *

Force

George Washington
Letter to Henry Lee October 31, 1786
If they have real grievances redress them, if possible; or acknowledge the justice of them, and your inability to do it at

the moment. If they have not, employ the force of government against them at once.

* * * * *

Benjamin Franklin
Poor Richard's Almanac
Force shits on reason's back.

* * * * *

Thomas Jefferson
Letter to papal nuncio Count Dugnani February 14, 1818
I have the consolation to reflect that during the period of my administration not a drop of the blood of a single fellow citizen was shed by the sword of war or of the law.

* * * * *

Forgiveness

Samuel Adams
Letter to Richard Henry Lee December 23, 1784
Great Britain, though she has concluded a Treaty of Peace with us, appears to be not a cordial Friend. She cannot forget her unparalleled Injustice towards us & naturally supposes there can be no Forgiveness on our Part.

This is similar to another quote of Adams' listed under "Compromise."

* * * * *

Forms of Government

Samuel Adams
Letter to Richard Henry Lee April 14, 1785
I firmly believe that the benevolent Creator designed the republican Form of Government for Man.

Will you venture so far as to say that all other Institutions that we know of are unnatural & tend more or less to distress human Societies?

Will the Lion ever associate with the Lamb or the Leopard with the Kid till our favorite principles shall be universally established?

* * * * *

John Adams
Letter to John Taylor April 15, 1814
Remember, democracy never lasts long. It soon wastes, exhausts, and murders itself. There never was a democracy yet that did not commit suicide.

* * * * *

John Adams
Letter to Thomas Jefferson November 13, 1815
The fundamental article of my political creed is that despotism, or unlimited sovereignty, or absolute power, is the same in a majority of a popular assembly, an aristocratic council, an oligarchic junta, and a single emperor. Equally arbitrary, cruel, bloody, and in every respect diabolical.

* * * * *

John Adams
Discourses on Davila 1790
The great art of law-giving consists in balancing the poor against the rich in the legislature, and in constituting the

legislative a perfect balance against the executive power, at the same time that no individual or party can become its rival.

The essence of a free government consists in an effectual control of rivalries. The executive and the legislative powers are natural rivals; and if each lacks an effectual control over the other, the weaker will forever be the lamb in the paws of the wolf.

The nation which will not adopt an equilibrium of power must adopt a despotism. There is no other alternative.

Rivalries must be controlled, or they will throw all things into confusion; and there is nothing but despotism or a balance of power which can control them.

* * * * *

Alexander Hamilton
Speech urging ratification of the U.S. Constitution June 21, 1788
It has been observed that a pure democracy if it were practicable would be the most perfect government. Experience has proved that no position is more false than this. The ancient democracies in which the people themselves deliberated never possessed one good feature of government. Their very character was tyranny; their figure deformity.

* * * * *

Alexander Hamilton
Debates for The Federal Constitution Jun 26, 1787
We are now forming a republican government. Real liberty is neither found in despotism or the extremes of democracy, but in moderate governments.

* * * * *

James Madison
Federalist #37
The genius of republican liberty seems to demand on one side, not only that all power should be derived from the

people, but that those entrusted with it should be kept dependent upon the people, by a short duration of their appointments; and that even during this short period the trust should be placed not in a few, but in a number of hands.

* * * * *

James Madison
Speech at the Virginia Convention to ratify the Federal Constitution June 6, 1788
Since the general civilization of mankind, I believe there are more instances of the abridgment of the freedom of the people by gradual and silent encroachments of those in power, than by violent and sudden usurpations.

But, on a candid examination of history, we shall find that turbulence, violence, and abuse of power, by the majority trampling on the rights of the minority, have produced factions and commotions, which, in republics, have, more frequently than any other cause, produced despotism.

If we go over the whole history of ancient and modern republics, we shall find their destruction to have generally resulted from those causes.

* * * * *

George Mason
Virginia Declaration of Rights 1776
Government is, or ought to be, instituted for the common benefit, protection, and security of the people, nation or community.

Of all the various modes and forms of government, that which is best, is that which is capable of producing the greatest degree of happiness and safety and is most effectually secured against the danger of maladministration…

Whenever any government shall be found inadequate or contrary to these purposes, a majority of the community hath an indubitable, unalienable, and indestructible right to reform, alter or abolish it, in such manner as shall be judged most conducive to the public weal.

"Weal" is an old word, meaning "well-being."

* * * * *

George Mason
Virginia Declaration of Rights 1776
The legislative and executive powers of the state should be separate and distinct from the judicial; and, that the members of the two first may be restrained from oppression by feeling and participating the burdens of the people, they should, at fixed periods, be reduced to a private station, returning into that body from which they were originally taken. And the vacancies be supplied by frequent, certain, and regular elections in which all, or any part of the former members, to be again eligible, or ineligible, as the laws shall direct.

* * * * *

George Mason
Virginia Declaration of Rights 1776
All power of suspending laws, or the execution of laws, by any authority without consent of the representatives of the people, is injurious to their rights and ought not to be exercised.

* * * * *

Patrick Henry
Virginia Ratifying Convention June 5, 1788
[Can you] show me that age and country where the rights and liberties of the people were placed on the sole chance of their rulers being good men, without a consequent loss of liberty?

* * * * *

Franklin's Virtues

Benjamin Franklin
His Autobiography, 1774

It was about this time I conceived the bold and arduous project of arriving at moral perfection. I wished to live without committing any fault at any time; I would conquer all that either natural inclination, custom, or company might lead me into.

As I knew, or thought I knew, what was right and wrong, I did not see why I might not always do the one and avoid the other.

But I soon found I had undertaken a task of more difficulty than I bad imagined. While my care was employed in guarding against one fault, I was often surprised by another; habit took the advantage of inattention; inclination was sometimes too strong for reason.

I concluded, at length, that the mere speculative conviction that it was our interest to be completely virtuous, was not sufficient to prevent our slipping; and that the contrary habits must be broken, and good ones acquired and established, before we can have any dependence on a steady, uniform rectitude of conduct. For this purpose I therefore contrived the following method.

In the various enumerations of the moral virtues I had met with in my reading, I found the catalogue more or less numerous, as different writers included more or fewer ideas under the same name. Temperance, for example, was by some confined to eating and drinking, while by others it was extended to mean the moderating every other pleasure, appetite, inclination, or passion, bodily or mental, even to our avarice and ambition.

I proposed to myself, for the sake of clearness, to use rather more names, with fewer ideas connected to each, than a few names with more ideas; and I included under thirteen names of virtues all that at that time occurred to me as necessary or desirable, and connected to each a short precept, which fully expressed the extent I gave to its meaning.

These names of virtues, with their precepts, were:

1. TEMPERANCE. Eat not to dullness; drink not to elevation.

2. SILENCE. Speak not but what may benefit others or yourself; avoid trifling conversation.

3. ORDER. Let all your things have their places; let each part of your business have its time.

4. RESOLUTION. Resolve to perform what you ought; perform without fail what you resolve.

5. FRUGALITY. Make no expense but to do good to others or yourself; i.e., waste nothing.

6. INDUSTRY. Lose no time; be always employed in something useful; cut off all unnecessary actions.

7. SINCERITY. Use no hurtful deceit; think innocently and justly, and, if you speak, speak accordingly.

8. JUSTICE. Wrong none by doing injuries, or omitting the benefits that are your duty.

9. MODERATION. Avoid extremes; forbear resenting injuries so much as you think they deserve.

10. CLEANLINESS. Tolerate no uncleanliness in body, clothes, or habitation.

11. TRANQUILLITY. Be not disturbed at trifles, or at accidents common or unavoidable.

12. CHASTITY. Rarely use sex but for health or offspring, never to dullness, weakness, or the injury of your own or another's peace or reputation.

13. HUMILITY. Imitate Jesus and Socrates.

My intention being to acquire the habitude of all these virtues, I judged it would be well not to distract my attention by attempting the whole at once, but to fix it on one of them at a time; and, when I should be master of that, then to proceed to another, and so on, till I should have gone through the thirteen; and, as the previous acquisition of some might facilitate the acquisition of certain others, I arranged them with that view, as they stand above.

Temperance first, as it tends to procure that coolness and clearness of head, which is so necessary where constant vigilance was to be kept up, and guard maintained against the unremitting attraction of ancient habits, and the force of perpetual temptations.

This being acquired and established, Silence would be more easy; and my desire being to gain knowledge at the same time that I improved in virtue, and considering that in conversation it was obtained rather by the use of the ears than of the tongue, and therefore wishing to break a habit I was getting into of prattling, punning, and joking, which only made me acceptable to insignificant company, I gave Silence the second place. This and the next, Order, I expected would allow me more time for attending to my project and my studies. Resolution, once become habitual, would keep me firm in my endeavors to obtain all the subsequent virtues; Frugality and Industry freeing me from my remaining debt, and producing affluence and independence, would make more easy the practice of Sincerity and Justice, etc., etc.

Conceiving then, that, agreeably to the advice of Pythagoras in his Golden Verses, daily examination would be necessary, I contrived the following method for conducting that examination.

I made a little book, in which I allotted a page for each of the virtues. I ruled each page with red ink, so as to have seven columns, one for each day of the week, marking each column with a letter for the day. I crossed these columns with thirteen red lines, marking the beginning of each line with the first letter of one of the virtues, on which line, and in its proper column, I might mark, by a little black spot, every fault I found upon examination to have been committed respecting that virtue upon that day.

* * * * *

Benjamin Franklin

His Autobiography, 1774

On the whole, though' I never arrived at the perfection I had been so ambitious of obtaining, but fell far short of it, yet I was, by the endeavor, a better and a happier man than I otherwise should have been if I had not attempted it.

* * * * *

Freedom of The Press

Thomas Jefferson

Conversation with Alexander von Humboldt June 1804

Humboldt (seeing a newspaper containing slanderous falsehoods against Jefferson on the President's desk):

> Why do you not have the fellow hung who dares to write these abominable lies?

Jefferson:

> What? Hang the guardians of the public morals? No, sir, - rather would I protect the spirit of freedom which dictates even that degree of abuse. Put that paper into your pocket, my good friend, carry it with you to Europe, and when you hear any one doubt the reality of American freedom, show them that paper, and tell them where you found it.

Humboldt:

> But is it not shocking that virtuous characters should be defamed?

Jefferson:

> Let their actions refute such libels. Believe me, virtue is not long darkened by the clouds of malice; and the temporary pain which it causes is infinitely overweighed by the safety it insures against degeneracy in the principles and conduct of public functionaries. When a man assumes a public trust, he should consider himself as public property.

George Mason

Virginia Declaration of Rights 1776

That the freedom of the press is one of the greatest bulwarks of liberty and can never be restrained, except by despotic governments.

* * * * *

James Madison

Report on the Virginia Resolutions, House of Representatives January 20, 1800

Some degree of abuse is inseparable from the proper use of every thing; and in no instance is this more true than in that of the press.

It has accordingly been decided, by the practice of the states, that it is better to leave a few of its noxious branches to their luxuriant growth, than, by pruning them away, to injure the vigor of those yielding the proper fruits.

And can the wisdom of this policy be doubted by any one who reflects that to the press alone, checkered as it is with abuses, the world is indebted for all the triumphs which have been gained by reason and humanity over error and oppression?

* * * * *

John Adams

Dissertation on Canon and Feudal Law, 1765

Liberty cannot be preserved without a general knowledge among the people, who have a right, from the frame of their nature, to knowledge, as their great Creator, who does nothing in vain, has given them understandings, and a desire to know.

But besides this, they have a right, an indisputable, unalienable, indefeasible, divine right to that most dreaded and envied kind of knowledge; I mean, of the characters and conduct of their rulers.

* * * * *

Freemen

George Washington
General Orders, July 2, 1776
Let us therefore animate and encourage each other, and show the whole world that a Freeman, contending for liberty on his own ground, is superior to any slavish mercenary on earth.

* * * * *

Friendship

Thomas Jefferson
The Life and Writings of Thomas Jefferson Published 1900
I never consider a difference of opinion in politics, in religion, in philosophy, as cause for withdrawing from a friend.

* * * * *

The Future of America

The founders had great hopes for the future of America, but also great worries. Following are quotes in that order:

George Washington
Letter to Francis Van der Kamp, May 28, 1788
I had always hoped that this land might become a safe and agreeable asylum to the virtuous and persecuted part of mankind, to whatever nation they might belong.

* * * * *

George Washington
Letter to the Marquis de Lafayette, June 19, 1788
I hope, some day or another, we shall become a storehouse and granary for the world.

* * * * *

Thomas Jefferson
Letter to E. Carrington 1788
The natural progress of things is for liberty to yield and government to gain ground.

Jefferson seems to be thinking that governments are permanent and cumulative structures and that humans are temporary beings who must slowly gain the wisdom to defend liberty. Also, perhaps, that the young are easily seduced by the promises of authorities.

* * * * *

Benjamin Franklin
Speech to the Constitutional Convention June 28, 1787
I agree to this Constitution, with all its faults, — if they are such; because I think a general Government necessary for us, and there is no form of government but what may be a blessing to the people, if well administered

And I believe, farther, that this is likely to be well administered for a course of years, and can only end in despotism, as other forms have done before it, when the people shall become so corrupted as to need despotic government, being incapable of any other.

* * * * *

Thomas Jefferson
Letter to John Holmes April 22, 1820
I regret that I am now to die in the belief, that the useless sacrifice of themselves by the generation of 1776, to acquire self-government and happiness to their country, is to be thrown away by the unwise and unworthy passions of their

sons, and that my only consolation is to be, that I live not to weep over it.

If they would but dispassionately weigh the blessings they will throw away, against an abstract principle more likely to be effected by union than by scission, they would pause before they would perpetrate this act of suicide on themselves, and of treason against the hopes of the world.

To yourself, as the faithful advocate of the Union, I tender the offering of my high esteem and respect.

* * * * *

Gain & Pain

Benjamin Franklin
Poor Richard's Almanac
Hope of gain, lessens pain.

* * * * *

The General Welfare

Madison, late in life, explains what he meant by "the general welfare."

James Madison
Letter to James Robertson April 20, 1831
With respect to the words "general welfare," I have always regarded them as qualified by the detail of powers connected with them. To take them in a literal and unlimited sense would be a metamorphosis of the Constitution into a character which, as is shown by a host of proofs, was not contemplated by its creators.

* * * * *

Thomas Jefferson
Letter to W. Giles, 1825
Aided by a little sophistry on the words 'general welfare', [they claim] a right to do not only the acts to effect that which are specifically enumerated and permitted, but whatsoever they shall think or pretend will be for the general welfare.

"Sophistry" refers to false and deceptive arguments; word-tricks.

* * * * *

God's Justice

Thomas Jefferson
Notes on the State of Virginia, 1781-1785
I tremble for my country when I reflect that God is just: that his justice cannot sleep for ever.

* * * * *

A Good Conscience

Benjamin Franklin
Poor Richard's Almanac
Let no Pleasure tempt thee, no Profit allure thee, no Ambition corrupt thee, no Example sway thee, no Persuasion move thee, to do any thing which you know to be Evil. By this you will always be happy: for a good Conscience is a continual Christmas.

* * * * *

Governance

Thomas Jefferson
Letter to Thomas Cooper November 29, 1802
If we can prevent the government from wasting the labors of the people, under the pretense of taking care of them, they must become happy.

* * * * *

Thomas Jefferson
Inaugural Address, March 4, 1801
A wise and frugal Government, which shall restrain men from injuring one another, shall leave them otherwise free to regulate their own pursuits of industry and improvement, and shall not take from the mouth of labor the bread it has earned.

This is the sum of good government, and this is necessary to close the circle of our felicities.

* * * * *

Thomas Jefferson
Letter to Francis W. Gilmer June 27, 1816
Every man is under the natural duty of contributing to the necessities of the society; and this is all the laws should enforce on him. And since no man has a natural right to be the judge between himself and another, it is his natural duty to submit to the umpiring of an impartial third.

When the laws have declared and enforced all this, they have fulfilled their functions, and the idea is quite unfounded, that on entering into society we give up any natural right.

Note that Jefferson uses the word "society" in the older way: Not "a society," implying an external set of rules he must conform to — but simply "society," meaning "a friendly association with others." This is an important distinction. Jefferson — as is obvious from the passage — does not think "society" requires any sacrifice of individual will.

Thomas Jefferson

Letter to William Ludlow September 6, 1824

I think myself that we have more machinery of government than is necessary, too many parasites living on the labor of the industrious.

* * * * *

John Adams

Letter to George Wythe April 1776

Fear is the foundation of most governments; but it is so sordid and brutal a passion, and renders men in whose breasts it predominates so stupid and miserable, that Americans will not be likely to approve of any political institution which is founded on it.

* * * * *

The Constitution opens with a statement that the people have chosen to create this government, and there are many similar statements throughout this collection of quotes. Here, however, Hamilton says that governments must be imposed upon men.

Alexander Hamilton

Federalist #15

Why has government been instituted at all? Because the passions of men will not conform to the dictates of reason and justice, without constraint.

* * * * *

Alexander Hamilton

Federalist #1

It has been frequently remarked that it seems to have been reserved to the people of this country, by their conduct and example, to decide the important question, whether societies of men are really capable or not of establishing good government from reflection and choice, or whether they are forever destined to depend for their political constitutions on accident and force.

* * * * *

Jay agrees with Hamilton.

John Jay
Federalist #2
Nothing is more certain than the indispensable necessity of government, and it is equally undeniable, that whenever and however it is instituted, the people must cede to it some of their natural rights in order to vest it with requisite powers.

* * * * *

Government Charity

James Madison
In the House of Representatives January 10, 1794
I cannot undertake to lay my finger on that article of the Constitution which granted a right to Congress of expending, on objects of benevolence [refugees from Haiti]… the money of their constituents.

The government of the United States is a definite government, confined to specified objects. It is not like the state governments, whose powers are more general. Charity is no part of the legislative duty of the government.

* * * * *

Government Debt

Thomas Jefferson

Letter to William Plumer July 21, 1816

I, however, place economy among the first and most important republican virtues, and public debt as the greatest of the dangers to be feared.

* * * * *

Thomas Jefferson

Letter to James Madison September 6, 1789

I say, the earth belongs to each of these generations during its course, fully and in its own right. The second generation receives it [the earth] clear of the debts and encumbrances of the first, the third of the second, and so on.

For if the first could charge it with a debt, then the earth would belong to the dead and not to the living generation.

Then, no generation can contract debts greater than may be paid during the course of its own existence.

* * * * *

Thomas Jefferson

Letter to John Taylor May 28, 1816

The principle of spending money to be paid by posterity, under the name of funding, is but swindling future generations on a large scale.

* * * * *

Thomas Jefferson

Letter to John Wayles Eppes 24 June 1813

The earth belongs to the living, not to the dead.

* * * * *

Alexander Hamilton

Letter to Robert Morris April 30, 1781

A national debt, if it is not excessive, will be to us a national blessing.

* * * * *

Alexander Hamilton

Alexander Hamilton's rise to prominence occurred during the Revolutionary War, where he served as George Washington's personal assistant. His intellectual gifts were evident to all who knew him (he had a remarkable ability to understand the essence of an issue, quickly, deeply and accurately), and several commanders sought him as an assistant. Hamilton held out until Washington noticed him, then accepted. He served Washington extremely well and earned his enduring trust, as this first passage displays: (Washington was a very loyal man.)

George Washington

1781

This I can venture to advance from a thorough knowledge of him, that there are few men to be found, of his age, who has a more general knowledge than he possesses, and none whose Soul is more firmly engaged in the cause, or who exceeds him in integrity and Sterling virtue.

* * * * *

During the revolution, Hamilton spoke eloquently in favor of natural rights.

Alexander Hamilton

The Farmer Refuted, 1775

The origin of all civil government, justly established, must be a voluntary compact, between the rulers and the ruled; and must be liable to such limitations, as are necessary for the security of the absolute rights of the latter; for what original title can any man or set of men have, to govern others, except their own consent?

To usurp dominion over a people, in their own despite, or to grasp at a more extensive power than they are willing to entrust, is to violate that law of nature, which gives every man a right to his personal liberty; and can, therefore, confer no obligation to obedience.

* * * * *

Alexander Hamilton
The Farmer Refuted 1775
The sacred rights of mankind are not to be rummaged for among old parchments or musty records. They are written, as with a sunbeam, in the whole volume of human nature, by the hand of the divinity itself; and can never be erased or obscured by mortal power.

* * * * *

As the war ended, Hamilton and congressmen Gouvernor Morris and Robert Morris (not related) took advantage of the Army's discontent (they had not been paid in a long time) and used the Newburgh Conspiracy of 1783 as leverage to give the national government the power to tax imports. (Taxes at this time were levied by each state, not by a central government.)

Hamilton and the congressmen worked secretly to encourage the rebellion and to force Congress to give in.

Hamilton wrote to Washington, suggesting that he covertly join and guide the rebellious Army officers, but the noble Washington wanted nothing to do with secret plots. Instead, he surprised the officers in one of their meetings and put an end to the plot. The officers backed-down, professed their loyalty, and went home.

This passage comes from a letter Washington wrote to the officers as he approached:

George Washington
Letter to Officers of the Army, March 12, 1783
Can you then consent to be the only sufferers by this revolution, and retiring from the field, grow old in poverty, wretchedness and contempt?

Can you consent to wade through the vile mire of dependency, and owe the miserable remnant of that life to charity, which has hitherto been spent in honor?

If you can - GO - and carry with you the jest of tories and scorn of whigs - the ridicule, and what is worse, the pity of the world. Go, starve, and be forgotten!

* * * * *

A few weeks after, Washington writes the following to Hamilton:

George Washington
Letter to Alexander Hamilton, April 4, 1783
The Army (considering the irritable state it is in, its suffering and composition) is a dangerous instrument to play with.

* * * * *

Afterward, Congress passed a measure for paying the Army without the central taxing scheme. Hamilton voted against it.

Then, Hamilton went to New York, studied for a few months, and was admitted to the New York Bar as a lawyer.

The next year, in 1784, he co-founded the Bank of New York and was fundamental to the founding of banking in the United States.

Hamilton was a delegate to the Constitutional Convention of 1787. The meeting in Philadelphia was supposed to be a mere revision to the Articles of Confederation, but Hamilton and James Madison (with others) succeeded in expanding their purpose. (There were some valid reasons for this. See Washington's comment in the section entitled "Constitution, Necessity of.") Nonetheless, several important people were absent: Thomas Jefferson was in Paris, John Adams was in London and Samuel Adams was in Boston.

But even Madison, who had worked with Hamilton to transform the meeting, complained about him, saying, essentially, that Hamilton had used him:

James Madison
The Records of the Federal Convention of 1787
I deserted Colonel Hamilton, or rather Colonel H. deserted me…

The divergence between us took place from his wishing to administration [wishing for control], or, rather, to administer [direct] the Government into what he thought it ought to be.

* * * * *

In promoting the new Constitution, Hamilton's arguments differed from his arguments of earlier days. He was no longer championing natural liberties and natural rights, but rather "the public good."

Alexander Hamilton
Federalist #1
Our choice should be directed by a judicious estimate of our true interests, unperplexed and unbiased by considerations not connected with the public good.

* * * * *

Here, Hamilton begins by characterizing his opposition as a would-be ruling class of power-grabbers, then concludes by saying that even if some of them had good intentions (not many people would have believed George Mason to be a power-grabber), they were deluded.

Alexander Hamilton
Federalist #1
Among the most formidable of the obstacles which the new Constitution will have to encounter may readily be distinguished the obvious interest of a certain class of men in every State to resist all changes which may hazard a diminution of the power, emolument, and consequence of the offices they hold under the State establishments; and the perverted ambition of another class of men, who will either hope to aggrandize themselves by the confusions of their

country, or will flatter themselves with fairer prospects of elevation from the subdivision of the empire into several partial confederacies than from its union under one government.

Candor will oblige us to admit that even such men may be actuated by upright intentions; and it cannot be doubted that much of the opposition which has made its appearance, or may hereafter make its appearance, will spring from sources, blameless at least, if not respectable--the honest errors of minds led astray by preconceived jealousies and fears. They are deluded and not respectable.

* * * * *

Here Hamilton argues directly that a powerful government is essential to liberty. Then he claims that zeal for the rights of the people is more dangerous than a zeal for a strong government.

Alexander Hamilton
Federalist #1

It will be equally forgotten that the vigor of government is essential to the security of liberty; that, in the contemplation of a sound and well-informed judgment, their interest can never be separated; and that a dangerous ambition more often lurks behind the specious mask of zeal for the rights of the people than under the forbidden appearance of zeal for the firmness and efficiency of government.

* * * * *

Once the Constitution was in place and Washington was elected President, Hamilton was appointed Secretary of the Treasury. He immediately went to work on two major plans: The Assumption of Debts and a central bank. The Assumption is addressed separately in this book (in a section of the same title), but it is important to reiterate that Hamilton and quite a few congressmen engaged in some very dirty dealing.

Madison wrote the following to Jefferson regarding the corruption of congressmen at this time:

James Madison
Letter to Thomas Jefferson July, 1791
Of all the shameful circumstances of this business, it is among the greatest to see the members of this legislature who were most active in pushing this job, openly grasping its profits.

* * * * *

Hamilton provided inside information in return for votes on his pet plans. Many congressmen and financial-industry friends bought up Revolutionary War debt at pennies on the dollar. These men knew in advance that it would soon be redeemed by the central government for full value, but no one else knew. They sent agents through hundreds of small towns and bought bonds from poor ex-soldiers for fractions of their stated value, then changed it in for full value as soon as the law was passed. One of the duped veterans wrote a letter to the Massachusetts Centinel on March 20, 1790, describing the situation of the Revolutionary War soldiers:

They must dispose of their... pay, or they must go hungry.

What was the encouragement when they offered their paper for sale? That government would never be able to pay it, and that it was not worth more than [ten percent of stated value].

* * * * *

To make things worse, Hamilton's Treasury Department erected near-impossible bureaucratic obstacle for individuals to redeem their debt paper, but made it easy for known dealers. At this time, the U.S. capital was New York, where Hamilton had his bank, where he met his friends for coffee, and where the Wall Street Dealers were then forming their first agreements to recognize each other (and no others) as authorized dealers in securities.

* * * * *

Jefferson, then Secretary of State, complains that he was duped by Hamilton:

Thomas Jefferson
Letter to George Washington August 9, 1792
I was duped ... by the Secretary of the treasury, and made a fool for forwarding his schemes, then insufficiently understood by me.

Of all the errors of my political life, this has occasioned the deepest regret.

* * * * *

John Adams was elected President in 1796, and he decided that it would be the right thing to retain Washington's cabinet. However, near then end of his term of office, in 1800, he found out that his cabinet members were obeying Hamilton rather than himself. He then fired James McHenry, Secretary of War and Timothy Pickering, Secretary of State.

At this time he called Hamilton "a man devoid of every moral principle."

* * * * *

Here is an illustrative story told by Jefferson:

Thomas Jefferson
Letter to Dr. Benjamin Rush 1811
I invited them to dine with me, and after dinner, sitting at our wine, having settled our question, other conversation came on, in which a collision of opinion arose between Mr. [John] Adams and Colonel [Alexander] Hamilton, on the merits of the British Constitution

Mr. Adams gave his opinion, that, if some of its defects and abuses were corrected, it would be the most perfect constitution of government ever devised by man. Hamilton, on the contrary, asserted that even with its existing vices, it was the most perfect model of government that could be formed; and that the correction of its vices would make it impracticable for government. And this you May be assured was the real line of difference between the political principles of these two gentlemen.

Another incident took place on the same occasion, which will further show Mr. Hamilton's political principles.

The room being hung around with a collection of the portraits of remarkable men, among them were those of Bacon, Newton and Locke.

Hamilton asked me who they were. I told him they were my trinity of the three greatest men the world had ever produced, naming them. He paused for some time: "The greatest man," said he, "that ever lived, was Julius Caesar."

Mr. Adams was honest as a politician as well as a man; Hamilton honest as a man, but, as a politician he believed in the necessity of either force or corruption to govern men.

* * * * *

Hamilton's Financial System

The Assumption was the first part of Hamilton's financial system. The second was a central bank – the Bank of The United States. This plan was passed by Congress in February, 1791, over the objections of Jefferson and Madison.

Like our current Federal Reserve Bank, the Bank of The United States was a private corporation chartered by Congress. It also dealt with money in complex processes which were unintelligible to most citizens.

The new bank got its capital partly from the new government and partly from private investors, some of whom paid with the same government bonds that Hamilton had issued at the Assumption.

To simplify this:

1. *The Treasury issued bonds to cover the Revolutionary War debt.*

2. *Many holders of the above bonds used them to purchase shares of the Bank of The United States. This saved the Treasury from having to pay out silver for them. (One dollar was then 371.25 grains of silver – a little more than ³/₄ of an ounce.)*

3. *The US government (via complicated arrangements) purchased shares of the Bank.*

4. *The bond-holders and the US government held only about 20% of the Bank's stock. The remaining 80% was sold to private individuals world-wide, through Wall Street dealers. (Only one-fourth of this was in silver or gold, the remainder being bonds, scrip, etc.)*

5. *The Bank was required to keep only 5% of its assets in "real money."*

6. *In order to pay interest on financial paper issued by the Bank, a new tax was required. (This led to the Whiskey Rebellion.)*

* * * * *

Here, Hamilton explains one of the mysteries of finance: How debt is turned into money:

Alexander Hamilton

Report on Public Credit January 9, 1790

It is a well known fact, that in countries in which the national debt is properly funded, and an object of established confidence, it answers most of the purposes of money. Transfers of stock or public debt are there equivalent to payments in specie [inherently valuable metal coins].

In other words, stock, in the principal transactions of business, passes current as specie.

Trade is extended by it; because there is a larger capital to carry it on, and the merchant can at the same time, afford to trade for smaller profits; as his stock, which, when unemployed, brings him in an interest from the government, serves him also as money, when he has a call for it in his commercial operations.

What Hamilton does not mention here is that the issuers of this debt must first get people to buy it. They do this by offering interest on the money. This interest is paid by taxing the populace.

To put this in simple terms: The holder of a government bond owns a right to the future earnings of the tax-payers.

Debt being used as money is a very significant issue. In fact, all current dollars in the United States are debt tokens.

* * * * *

Here is Jefferson's explanation of how Hamilton corrupted the congress:

Thomas Jefferson
The Anas, 1818

Hamilton's financial system had then passed. It had two objects:

- First, as a puzzle, to exclude popular understanding and inquiry.

- Secondly, as a machine for the corruption of the Legislature.

Hamilton had avowed the opinion, that man could be governed by one of two motives only, force or interest. Force, he observed, in this country was out of the question; and the interests, therefore, of the members must be laid hold of, to keep the Legislature in unison with the Executive.

And with grief and shame it must be acknowledged that his machine was not without effect; that even in this, the birth of our government, some members were found dirty enough to bend their duty to their interests, and to look after personal, rather than public good.

The measures of Hamilton's financial system, -- the Funding and United States Bank Acts added to the number of votaries [sycophants] to the Treasury, and made its Chief the master of every vote in the Legislature, which might give to the government the direction suited to his political views.

I know well... that nothing like a majority in Congress had yielded to this corruption. Far from it. But a division, not very unequal, had already taken place in the honest part of that body, between the parties styled republican and federal. The latter being monarchists in principle, adhered to Hamilton of course, as their leader in that principle, and this mercenary phalanx added to them, ensured him always a majority in both Houses; so that the whole action of the Legislature was now under the direction of the Treasury.

By this combination, legislative explanations were given to the Constitution, and all the administrative laws were shaped on the model of England, and so passed.

Here then was the real ground of the opposition which was made to the course of administration. Its object was to preserve the Legislature pure and independent of the Executive, to limit the administration to republican forms and principles, and not permit the Constitution to be construed into a monarchy, and to be warped in practice into all the principles and pollutions of their favorite English model.

Nor was this an opposition to General Washington. He was true to the republican charge confided to him; and has solemnly and repeatedly protested to me, in our conversations that he would lose the last drop of his blood in support of it; and he did this the oftener, and with the more earnestness, because he knew my suspicions of Hamilton's designs against it, and wished to quiet them. For he was not aware of the drift, or of the effect of Hamilton's schemes. Unversed in financial projects, and calculations and budgets, his approval of them was based on his confidence in the man [Hamilton].

* * * * *

Here, Jefferson opines that Congress has no power to establish the Bank:

Thomas Jefferson
Opinion on creating a National Bank 1791
The incorporation of a bank, and the powers assumed by this bill... are not among the powers specially enumerated [to Congress in the Constitution].

* * * * *

And Hamilton argues for a very broad interpretation of government powers, including the chartering of the Bank. He says that since his opponents do admit that there are implied powers, the plain language of the Constitution is overridden by them.

Alexander Hamilton
For The Bank February 23, 1791

Every power vested in a government is in its nature sovereign and includes, by force of the term, a right to employ all the Means requisite and fairly applicable to the attainment of the Ends of such power, and which are not precluded by restrictions and exceptions specified in the Constitution, or not immoral, or contrary to the essential ends of political society...

The first of these arguments [against the power of the government to erect corporations] is that the foundation of the Constitution is laid on this ground: "that all powers not delegated to the United States by the Constitution, nor prohibited to it by the states, are reserved for the states, or to the people." This is meant to infer that Congress can in no case exercise any power [that is not] enumerated in the Constitution. And it is affirmed that the power of erecting a corporation is not included in any of the enumerated powers....

It is not denied that there are implied as well as express powers and that the former are as effectually delegated as the latter.... Then it follows that as a power of erecting a corporation may as well be implied as any other thing, it may as well be employed as an instrument or mean of carrying into execution any of the specified powers as any other instrument or mean whatever.

A criterion of what is constitutional and of what is not... is the purpose to which the measure relates as a method.

If the purpose is clearly comprehended within any of the specified powers, and if the method has an obvious relation to that end, and is not forbidden by a particular provision of the Constitution, it may safely be deemed to come within the compass of the national authority.

A bank relates to the collection of taxes in two ways -- indirectly, by increasing the quantity of circulating medium and quickening circulation, which facilitates the methods of paying directly, by creating a convenient species of medium in which they are to be paid. To designate or appoint the Money or Thing in which taxes are to be paid is not only a proper but a Necessary Exercise of the power of collecting them.... The appointment, then, of the Money or Thing in which the taxes are to be paid is an incident to the power of collection.

Notice Hamilton's argument that "If the purpose... is not forbidden by a particular provision of the Constitution, it... comes within the compass of the national authority." Complicated language aside, this is the opposite principle to the Bill of Rights, and to the Constitution in general.

The Constitution lists specific powers that the people grant to the corporation called the United States government, and the government was given no others. To seize other powers would be to violate their charter. The Bill of Rights (part of the Constitution) continues this by specifically listing things Congress may not do.

Note the opposing principles:

- *The Constitution: Congress can do only those things which are permitted.*

- *Hamilton: Congress can do anything that is not forbidden.*

To conclude this issue: If Congress at any time thought that more powers were needed for some important, practical reason, an honest path was always open to them: They could have passed an amendment.

* * * * *

Happiness

George Washington
Letter to Mary Ball Washington, May 15, 1787
Happiness depends more upon the internal frame of a person's own mind, than on the externals in the world.

* * * * *

Benjamin Franklin
Autobiography 1787
Human happiness is produced not so much by great pieces of good fortune that seldom happen, as by little advantages that occur every day.

* * * * *

Heretics

Benjamin Franklin
Letter to Benjamin Vaughan October 24, 1788
I think all the heretics I have known have been virtuous men.

They have the virtue of fortitude or they would not venture forward in their heresy.

And they cannot afford to be deficient in any of the other virtues, as that would give an advantage to their many enemies; and they lack, as do orthodox sinners, a number of friends to excuse or justify them.

Do not, however mistake me. It is not to my good friend's heresy that I impute his honesty. On the contrary, it is his honesty that has brought upon him the character of heretic.

* * * * *

High Office

George Washington
Letter to Catherine Macaulay Graham January 9, 1790
All see, and most admire, the glare which hovers round the external trappings of elevated office.

To me there is nothing in it, beyond the luster which may be reflected from its connection with a power of promoting human happiness.

* * * * *

Honesty

George Washington
Farewell Address September 17, 1796
I hold the maxim no less applicable to public than to private affairs, that honesty is always the best policy.

* * * * *

Honor

Honor is demonstrated in action, not in promises. The first of these quotes is a letter from Sam Adams to his friends Elbridge Gerry and James Lowell. The three are combining their efforts to look after the children of their deceased friend.

Samuel Adams
Letter to Elbridge Gerry And James Lovell December 20, 1779
Since my last Letter to you, I have had an Opportunity of conversing with Doctor John Warren, Brother of our deceased Friend, concerning the Situation of his Children.

He tells me that the eldest son was, as fairly as it could be done, put under the Care and Tuition of the Reverend Mr. Payson of Chelsea; a Gentleman whose Qualifications for the instructing of Youth, I need not mention to you. The Lad still remains with him.

The eldest Daughter, a Miss of about thirteen, is with the Doctor; and he assures me, that no Gentleman's Daughter in this Town has more of the Advantage of Schools than she has at his Expense. She learns Music, Dancing, writing & Arithmetic, and the best Needle Work that is taught here. The Doctor, I dare say, takes good Care of her Morals.

The two younger Children, a Boy of about seven years, and a Girl somewhat older, are in the Family of John Scollay Esquire, under the particular Care of his Daughter at her most earnest Request; otherwise, I suppose, they would have been taken Care of by their Relations at Roxbury, and educated as reputable Farmers Children usually are.

Miss Scollay deserves the greatest Praise for her Attention to them. She is exceedingly well qualified for her Charge; and her Affection for their deceased Father prompts her to exert her utmost to inculcate in the Minds of these Children, those Principles which may conduce, "to render them worthy of the Relation they stood in" to him.

General Arnold has assisted, by generously ordering five hundred Dollars towards their Support. This I was informed of when I was last in Philadelphia. I called on him & thanked him for his Kindness to them. Whether he has done more for them since, I cannot say. Probably he originated the subscription you have mentioned to me.

* * * * *

This great profession was followed by actions, as we know.

Thomas Jefferson
Declaration of Independence 1776
For the support of this declaration, with a firm reliance on the protection of divine providence, we mutually pledge to each other our lives, our fortunes, and our sacred honor.

* * * * *

Hope

Benjamin Franklin
Poor Richard's Almanac
He that lives upon Hope, dies fasting.

* * * * *

Patrick Henry
Second Virginia Convention March 23, 1775

It is natural to man to indulge in the illusions of hope. We are apt to shut our eyes against a painful truth, and listen to the song of that siren till she transforms us into beasts.

* * * * *

Humility

Thomas Jefferson
Letter to Rev. William Smith, 1791

The succession to Doctor Franklin, at the court of France, was an excellent school of humility.

On being presented to any one as the minister of America, the commonplace question used in such cases was "c'est vous, Monsieur, qui remplace le Docteur Franklin"? "It is you, sir, who replace Doctor Franklin"?

I generally answered, "no one can replace him, sir; I am only his successor".

* * * * *

Idolatry

Samuel Adams
Letter to Elbridge Gerry November 27, 1780

Mankind is prone enough to political Idolatry.

* * * * *

Immunization

Benjamin Franklin
On Immunization
In 1736 I lost one of my sons, a fine boy of four years old, by the small-pox, taken in the common way. I long regretted bitterly and still regret that I had not given it to him by inoculation. This I mention for the sake of parents who omit that operation on the supposition that they should never forgive themselves if a child died under it, by example showing that the regret may be the same either way and that, therefore, the safer should be chosen.

* * * * *

Improvement

Samuel Adams
Letter to Samuel Cooper April 30, 1776
We cannot make Events. Our Business is wisely to improve them.

There has been much to do to confirm doubting Friends & fortify the Timid. It requires time to bring honest Men to think and determine alike even in important Matters.

Mankind are governed more by their feelings than by reason.

* * * * *

Indians

Sam Adams maintains that the Indians posses rights from God.

Samuel Adams
Boston Gazaette, February 1, 1773
[We must consider the state of the] English North American
continent at the time, when, and after possession was first
taken of any part of it, by the Europeans. It was then
possessed by heathen and barbarous people, who had,
nevertheless, all that right to the soil, and sovereignty in and
over the lands they possessed, which God had originally
given to man.

* * * * *

*Sam Adams writes to the Mohawk Indians at the beginning of the Revolutionary
War:*

Samuel Adams
Address Of Massachusetts To Mohawk Indians March, 1775
Brothers-- We, the delegates of the inhabitants of the
Province of the Massachusetts Bay, being come together to
consider what may be best for you and ourselves to do, in
order to get ourselves rid of those hardships which we feel
and fear, have thought it our duty to tell you, our good
brothers, what our fathers in Great Britain have done and
threaten to do with us.

Brothers--You have heard how our fathers were obliged by
the cruelty of their brethren to leave their country; how they
crossed the great lake and came here; how they purchased
this land with their own money; and how, since that time,
they and we, their sons and grandsons, have built our houses
and cut down the trees, and cleared and improved the land at
their and our own expense; how we have fought for them,
and conquered Canada and a great many other places which

they have had and have not paid for; after all which and many other troubles, we thought we had reason to hope that they would be kind to us, and allow us to enjoy ourselves, and sit in our own houses, and eat our own victuals in peace and quiet; but alas! our brothers, we are greatly distressed, and we will tell you our grief; for you, as well as we, are in danger.

Brothers--Our fathers in Great Britain tell us our land and houses and cattle and money are not our own; that we ourselves are not our own men, but their servants; they have endeavored to take away our money without our leave, and have sent their great vessels and a great many warriors for that purpose.

Brothers--We used to send our vessels on the great lake, whereby we were able to get clothes and what we needed for ourselves and you; but such has lately been their conduct that we cannot; they have told us we shall have no more guns, no powder to use, and kill our wolves and other game, nor to send to you for you to kill your food with, and to get skins to trade with us, to buy your blankets and what you want. How can you live without powder and guns? But we hope to supply you soon with both, of our own making.

Brothers--They have made a law to establish the religion of the Pope in Canada, which lies so near you. We much fear some of your children may be induced, instead of worshipping the only true God, to pay His dues to images made with their own hands.

Brothers--These and many other hardships we are threatened with, which, no doubt, in the end will equally affect you; for the same reason they would get our lands, they would take away yours. All we want is that we and you may enjoy that liberty and security which we have a right to enjoy, and that we may not lose that good land which enables us to feed our wives and children. We think it our duty to inform you of our danger, and desire you to give notice to all your kindred; and as we much fear they will attempt to cut our throats, and if you should allow them to do that, there will nobody remain to keep them from you, we therefore earnestly desire you to whet your hatchet, and be prepared with us to defend our liberties and lives.

Brothers--We humbly beseech that God who lives above, and does what is right here below, to enlighten your minds to see that you ought to endeavor to prevent our fathers from bringing those miseries upon us; and to his good providence we commend you.

* * * * *

Samuel Adams
Letter to John Adams, December 20, 1780
The old Gentleman tells me that…

He says, that the Creeks & the Choctaws, which are the most numerous tribes of Indians, consisting of at least 8 perhaps 10 thousand Gun men, are our staunch Friends. The Heads of them have lately spoken to him in this Language, "We stand on the same Ground with you, we drink the same Water, breathe the same Air.. you are the Buds, & can there be Fruit if the Buds are nipped off?"

These are forcible Words, which express their own Sense of the Necessity of their Union with us for their very Existence. They are a sagacious as well as a powerful People, & an Alliance & Friendship with them is of Importance to all the United States.

* * * * *

Thomas Jefferson
Letter to Benjamin Hawkins August 13, 1786
The two principles on which our conduct towards the Indians should be founded, are justice and fear. After the injuries we have done them, they cannot love us.

* * * * *

Independence

Samuel Adams
Speech in Philadelphia August 1, 1776

Did the protection we received annul our rights as men, and lay us under an obligation of being miserable? Who among you, my countrymen, that is a father, would claim authority to make your child a slave because you had nourished him in infancy?

* * * * *

Industrial Economy, Transition To

James Madison
Quoted by Robert Yates June 26, 1787

The man who is possessed of wealth, who lolls on his sofa or rolls in his carriage, cannot judge the wants or feelings of the day-laborer.

The government we mean to erect is intended to last for ages. The landed interest, at present, is prevalent; but in process of time, when we approximate to the states and kingdoms of Europe, — when the number of landholders shall be comparatively small, through the various means of trade and manufactures, will not the landed interest be overbalanced in future elections, and unless wisely provided against, what will become of your government?

* * * * *

Ingratitude

George Washington
Letter to Governor Dinwiddie May 29, 1754
Nothing is a greater stranger to my breast, or a sin that my soul more abhors, than that black and detestable one, ingratitude.

* * * * *

Intelligence

Samuel Adams
Letter to James Lovell March 25, 1780
I thank you for the Intelligence you enclosed, and have made a prudent use of it, by communicating it to some of the leading members of the Assembly who are my confidential Friends. To others I have given it in my own way as Articles of my political Creed, and I think to good Effect.

* * * * *

Samuel Adams
Letter to Stephan Collins January 31, 1775
Our "worthy citizen" Mr. Paul Revere will explain to you the intelligence which we have just received from England. It puts me in mind of what I remember to have heard you observe, that we may all be soon under the necessity of keeping shooting irons.

God grant that we may not be brought to extremity or otherwise prepare us for all events.

* * * * *

Samuel Adams
Letter to Elbridge Geary September 16, 1775
I write you this letter, principally to put you in mind of the promise you made me to give me intelligence of what is doing in our assembly and the camp. Believe me, Sir, it is of great importance that we should be informed of every circumstance of our affairs.

We were told here that there were none in our camp who understood the business of an engineer, or any thing more than the manual exercise of the gun. This we had from great authority, and for want of more certain intelligence were obliged at least to be silent.

There are many military geniuses at present unemployed and overlooked, who I hope, when the army is new modeled, will be sought after and invited into the service of their country.

They must be sought after, for modest merit declines pushing itself into public view.

* * * * *

Intentions Versus Results

Benjamin Franklin
Letter to his father April 13, 1738
I think opinions should be judged by their influences and effects, and if a man holds none that tend to make him less virtuous or more vicious, it may be concluded that he holds none that are dangerous; which I hope is the case with me.

* * * * *

Interpreting The Constitution

Sam Adams argues that the end (that is, the goal) of any good constitution is liberty (he mentions the English and Massachusetts constitutions in particular), and that all questions must be decided with that goal in mind. He goes on to say that any interpretation which subverts liberty is a false interpretation of a document written with the over-riding goal of maintaining it.

Samuel Adams
Boston Gazette, January 20, 1772

The English constitution, says Baron Montesquieu, has Liberty for its direct object: And the constitution of this province, as our own historian informs us, is an epitome of the British constitution; and it undoubtedly has the same end for its object:

Whatever laws therefore are made for our government, in any way subversive of Liberty, must be subversive of the goal of the constitution, and consequently of the constitution itself.

* * * * *

Samuel Adams
Letter to Richard Henry Lee August 29, 1789

What have the United States been contending for? Liberty. This is the great Object of their State Governments, and has not the federal Constitution the same Object in View?

If therefore a Doubt arises respecting the Exercise of any Power, no Construction, I conceive, should militate with the main Design, or Object of the Charter.

* * * * *

Thomas Jefferson
Letter to William Johnson, 1823

On every question of construction, [we should] carry ourselves back to the time when the Constitution was adopted, recollect the spirit manifested in the debates, and instead of trying what meaning may be squeezed out of the text, or invented against it, conform to the probable one in which it was passed.

* * * * *

Hamilton argues differently than Adams — not that liberty should to be served above all, but that rules are to be interpreted and extended: That real-world considerations are to be secondary to written rules.

Alexander Hamilton
Opinion on the Constitutionality of the Bank February 23, 1791
Every power vested in a government is in its nature sovereign, and includes by force of the term a right to employ all the means requisite...to the attainment of the ends of such power...

If the goal be clearly comprehended within any of the specified powers, and if the measure have an obvious relation to that end, and is not forbidden by any particular provision of the Constitution, it may safely be deemed to come within the compass of the national authority.

* * * * *

Jefferson's Cannons For Practical Life

Jefferson, a very old man, offers his religious and moral creed to the son of a friend.

Thomas Jefferson
Letter to the infant Thomas Jefferson Smith, February 21, 1825
This letter will, to you, be as one from the dead. The writer will be in the grave before you can weigh its counsels.

Your affectionate and excellent father has requested that I would address to you something which might possibly have a favorable influence on the course of the life you have to run, and I too, as a namesake, feel an interest in that course. Few words will be necessary with good tendencies on your part.

Adore God. Reverence and cherish your parents. Love your neighbor as yourself, and your country more than yourself. Be just. Be true. Murmur not at the ways of Providence. So shall the life into which you have entered be the portal to one of eternal and indescribable bliss.

And if the dead are permitted to care for the things of this world, every action of your life will be under my regard. Farewell.

A Decalogue of Canons for Observation in Practical Life

1. Never put off till to-morrow what you can do today.

2. Never trouble another for what you can do yourself.

3. Never spend your money before you have it.

4. Never buy what you do not want, because it is cheap; it will be dear to you.

5. Pride costs us more than hunger, thirst and cold.

6. We never repent of having eaten too little.

7. Nothing is troublesome that we do willingly.

8. Much pain comes to us over evils which will never happen.

9. Take things always by their smooth handle.

10. When angry, count ten before you speak; if very angry, an hundred.

* * * * *

Jefferson & Adams

Thomas Jefferson and John Adams had a difficult relationship. Friendly during the revolution, they became alienated during the political campaigns of 1796 and 1800, as well as during their Presidencies. It was some years after that their mutual friend, Dr. Benjamin Rush, started them corresponding again. After that point, they remained devoted to each other for the rest of their lives.

John Adams
Letter to Benjamin Rush June 21, 1811
[The Declaration of Independence] I always considered as a Theatrical Show. Jefferson ran away with all the stage effect of that; i.e. all the Glory of it.

Contrast this quote with the one listed under "Declaration of Independence," written at the time.

* * * * *

John Adams
Letter to Thomas Jefferson June 28, 1813
The general principles on which the fathers achieved independence, were ... the general principles of Christianity, in which all those sects were united, and the general principles of English and American liberty, in which all those young men united, and which had united all parties in America, in majorities sufficient to assert and maintain her independence.

* * * * *

John Adams
Letter to Thomas Jefferson July 13, 1813
You and I ought not to die before we have explained ourselves to each other.

* * * * *

Jesus

Benjamin Franklin
Letter to Ezra Stiles, March 9, 1790

As to Jesus of Nazareth, my Opinion of whom you particularly desire, I think the System of Morals and his Religion, as he left them to us, is the best the World ever saw, or is likely to see.

* * * * *

Thomas Jefferson
Letter to Benjamin Rush April 12, 1803

[Of Jesus…] His parentage was obscure; his condition poor; his education null; his natural endowments great; his life correct and innocent: he was meek, benevolent, patient, firm, disinterested, and of the sublimest eloquence…

All the learned of his country, entrenched in its power and riches, were opposed to him, lest his labors should undermine their advantages; and the committing to writing his life & doctrines fell on the most unlettered & ignorant men; who wrote, too, from memory, & not till long after the transactions had passed…

His moral doctrines, relating to kindred & friends, were more pure & perfect than those of the most correct of the philosophers, and greatly more so than those of the Jews; and they went far beyond both in inculcating universal philanthropy, not only to kindred and friends, to neighbors and countrymen, but to all mankind, gathering all into one family, under the bonds of love, charity, peace, common wants and common aids.

A development of this reasoning will reveal the peculiar superiority of the system of Jesus over all others…

The precepts of philosophy, & of the Hebrew code, laid hold of actions only. He pushed his examinations into the heart of man; erected his tribunal in the region of his thoughts, and purified the waters at the fountain head.

The Jews

John Adams, a religious man, had specific thoughts regarding the Jews.

John Adams
Letter to François Adriaan van der Kemp February 16, 1809
I will insist that the Hebrews have done more to civilize men than any other nation. If I were an atheist, and believed in blind eternal fate, I should still believe that fate had ordained the Jews to be the most essential instrument for civilizing the nations.

If I were an atheist of the other sect, who believe or pretend to believe that all is ordered by chance, I should believe that chance had ordered the Jews to preserve and propagate to all mankind the doctrine of a supreme, intelligent, wise, almighty sovereign of the universe, which I believe to be the great essential principle of all morality, and consequently of all civilization.

* * * * *

John Adams
Letter to Mordecai Manuel Noah 1819
I really wish the Jews again in Judea, an independent nation, for, as I believe, the most enlightened men of it have participated in the amelioration of the philosophy of the age; once restored to an independent government, and no longer persecuted, they would soon wear away some of the asperities and peculiarities of their character, possibly in time become liberal Unitarian Christians, for your Jehovah is our Jehovah, and your God of Abraham, Isaac, and Jacob is our God.

* * * * *

Joint Cause

Samuel Adams
Boston Gazette, September 16, 1771

The cause of one is the cause of all. If the parliament may lawfully deprive New-York of any of its Rights, it may deprive any or all the other Colonies of their Rights; and nothing can so much encourage such attempts, as a mutual inattention to the interests of each other.

To divide and thus to destroy, is the first political maxim in attacking those who are powerful by their union. When Mr. Hampden's ship money cause for three shillings and four pence was tried, all the people of England, with anxious expectation, interested themselves in the important decision: And when the slightest point touching the freedom of a single Colony is agitated, I earnestly wish, that all the rest may with equal ardor support their sister.

These are the generous sentiments of that celebrated writer, whom several have made feeble attempts to answer, but no one has yet done it.

May the British American Colonies be upon their guard; and take care lest by a mutual inattention to the interest of each other, they at length become supine and careless of the grand cause of American Liberty, and finally fall a prey to the merciless hand of tyranny.

* * * * *

Judges

Thomas Jefferson
Letter to Thomas Cooper 1810

Knowing that religion does not furnish grosser bigots than law, I expect little from old judges.

* * * * *

The Judiciary

Thomas Jefferson
Letter to Thomas Ritchie December 25, 1820

The judiciary of the United States is the subtle corps of sappers and miners constantly working underground to undermine the foundations of our confederated fabric.

They are interpreting and changing our constitution from a coordination of a general and special government to a general and supreme one alone. This will lay all things at their feet, and they are too well versed in English law to forget the maxim, boni judicis est ampliare juris-dictionem. [A good judge increases his jurisdiction.]

We shall see if they are bold enough to take the daring stride their five lawyers have lately taken. If they do, then, with the editor of our book, in his address to the public, I will say, that "against this every man should raise his voice," and more, should uplift his arm.

Who wrote this admirable address? Sound, luminous, strong, not a word too much, nor one which can be changed but for the worse. That pen should go on, lay bare these wounds of our constitution, expose the decisions in succession, and arouse, as it is able, the attention of the nation to these bold speculators on its patience.

Having found, from experience, that impeachment is an impracticable thing, a mere scare-crow, they consider themselves secure for life; they skulk from responsibility to public opinion, the only remaining hold on them, under a practice first introduced into England by Lord Mansfield.

An opinion is huddled up in conclave, perhaps by a majority of one, delivered as if unanimous, and with the silent acquiescence of lazy or timid associates, by a crafty chief judge, who sophisticates the law to his mind, by the turn of his own reasoning.

* * * * *

John Adams
Letter to George Wythe April 1776
The judicial power ought to be distinct from both the legislative and executive, and independent upon both, that so it may be a check upon both, as both should be checks upon that.

* * * * *

The Constitution does not make the Supreme Court its official interpreter. That role began as a politically-influenced decision in 1803, called Marbury v. Madison. In this decision, the court actually ruled against James Madison, the primary author of the Constitution, and claimed the sole right to interpret that document. Here, Jefferson, a sitting President, objects:

Thomas Jefferson
Letter to Abigail Adams 1804
The Constitution... meant that its coordinate branches should be checks on each other. But the opinion which gives to the judges the right to decide what laws are constitutional and what not, not only for themselves in their own sphere of action but for the Legislature and Executive also in their spheres, would make the Judiciary a despotic branch.

* * * * *

Juries

The proper duties of juries has changed and been disputed over time. (In Medieval England, juries were composed of witnesses.) In this first quote, Sam Adams dislikes the fact that jurors are being brought in from some distance, that they do not know the witness, and are unable to judge their characters.

Samuel Adams
Boston Gazette, Dec. 11, 1770

Witnesses who are brought into a court of justice, while their veracity is not impeached, stand equal in the eye of the judge; unless he happens to be acquainted with their different characters, which is not presumed.

The jury who are taken from the vicinity, are supposed to know the credibility of the witnesses: In the late trials the witnesses were most, if not all of them, either inhabitants of this town or transient persons residing in it, and the jurors were all from the country: Therefore it is not likely that they were acquainted with the characters of all the witnesses; and it is more than probable that in so great a number of witnesses there were different characters, that is, that some of them were more, others less creditable.

If then the judge, whose province it is to attend to the law, and who, not knowing the characters of the witnesses, presumes that they are all good, & gives an equal credit to them, it is the duty of the jurors who are sovereign in regard to facts, to determine in their own minds the credibility of those who are sworn to relate the facts.

* * * * *

In the following passage, John Jay, then Chief Justice of the Supreme Court, explicitly approves of "jury nullification," which is the right of the jury to judge not only the facts, but the law. In other words, a jury has every right to ignore the law if they don't like it, and serves as the final protection against tyranny. This ruling has been assaulted by the US justice system ever since, but never overturned. In 1895, in a case named Sparf v. United States, the Court ruled that jurors may be kept ignorant of this right, but the right itself remains.

John Jay
Georgia v. Brailsford, 1794
It is presumed, that juries are the best judges of facts; it is, on the other hand, presumed that courts are the best judges of law. But still both objects are within your power of decision... you [the jury] have a right to take it upon yourselves to judge both, and to determine the law as well as the fact in controversy.

* * * * *

The Law & Laws

The original law of England was the "common law," and it had absolutely nothing to do with legislation. Law was defined and clarified in specific cases, not by members of Parliament, but by judges. This makes conversations about the law confusing: Judges clarified and discovered law in the old days of the common law; in our times, legislatures make laws.

Samuel Adams
Boston Gazette, August 20, 1770.
I confess that "too great a respect cannot be paid to the honorable part of the profession of the law," but when state-lawyers, attorneys and solicitors general, and persons advanced to the highest stations in the courts of law, prostitute the honor of the profession, become tools of ministers, and employ their talents for explaining away, if possible the Rights of a kingdom, they are then the proper objects of the contempt and anger of the public.

* * * * *

Below, the civil law Adams refers to is the more European form of law, built on a different theory of rights.

Common law was founded on "negative rights" – you are free to do whatever you wish, so long as you don't transgress known law.

Civil law was founded on positive "rights" – you are free to do only what the law specifically permits.

Samuel Adams
Letter to Arthur Lee September 27, 1771
"The Conduct of the Judges touching Juries" appears to be alarming on both sides of the water & ought to be strictly enquired into.

And are they not establishing the civil Law which Mr. Blackstone says is only permitted in England by dismissing the Common Law?

Blackstone wrote esteemed commentaries on the common law; they were best-sellers in the colonies.

* * * * *

Samuel Adams
Boston Gazette, January 20, 1772
Mr. Hooker in his ecclesiastical policy, as quoted by Mr. Locke, affirms that "Laws they are not, which the public approbation hath not made so."

This seems to be the language of nature and common sense; for if the public are bound to yield obedience to the laws, to which they cannot give their approval, they are slaves to those who make such laws and enforce them.

* * * * *

Samuel Adams
Independent Chronicle, January 19, 1795
If we continue to be a happy people, that happiness must be assured by the enacting and executing of reasonable and wise laws, expressed in the plainest language.

* * * * *

Madison points to a critical issue: If law cannot be relied upon (since it may change in the next session of congress), many commercial activities become risky and uncertain.

James Madison
Federalist #62, 1788
It will be of little avail to the people that the laws are made by men of their own choice, if the laws are so voluminous that they cannot be read, or so incoherent that they cannot be understood; if they be repealed or revised before they are promulgated, or undergo such incessant changes that no man who knows what the law is today can guess what it will be to-morrow.

* * * * *

Thomas Jefferson
Inaugural Address, March 4, 1801
I believe it [the US government] is the only one where every man, at the call of the laws, would fly to the standard of the law, and would meet invasions of the public order as his own personal concern.

* * * * *

Thomas Jefferson
Letter to Francis W. Gilmer June 27, 1816
No man has a natural right to commit aggression on the equal rights of another; and this is all from which the laws ought to restrain him.

Thomas Jefferson

Letter to Isaac H. Tiffany 1819

Rightful liberty is unobstructed action according to our will within limits drawn around us by the equal rights of others. I do not add "within the limits of the law" because law is often but the tyrant's will, and always so when it violates the rights of the individual.

* * * * *

Here, the astute Hamilton expresses a clear thought that is often bypassed: All laws are authorizations of violence. As Hamilton notes, a law without force is merely a suggestion. People who ask for laws are asking for violence to be used in specified circumstances.

Alexander Hamilton

Federalist #15

Government implies the power of making laws. It is essential to the idea of a law, that it be attended with a sanction; or, in other words, a penalty or punishment for disobedience.

If there be no penalty annexed to disobedience, the resolutions or commands which pretend to be laws will, in fact, amount to nothing more than advice or recommendation.

This penalty, whatever it may be, can only be inflicted in two ways: by the agency of the courts and ministers of justice, or by military force; by the Coercion of the magistracy, or by the Coercion of arms.

* * * * *

While all of the founders had a certain respect for the Constitution (even those who thought it went too far), Hamilton holds it sacred, as the fount of virtues. Other founders held virtue to be the root and the Constitution to be its produce. (Or, if Jefferson's estimation of Hamilton was correct, this is merely a statement for public consumption, to make people malleable and obedient.)

Alexander Hamilton

Essay in the American Daily Advertiser August 28, 1794

If it be asked, What is the most sacred duty and the greatest source of our security in a Republic? The answer would be: An inviolable respect for the Constitution and Laws — the first growing out of the last...

A sacred respect for the constitutional law is the vital principle, the sustaining energy of a free government.

* * * * *

Liberty

Samuel Adams

Boston Gazette, October 28, 1771

Every man was born naturally free; nothing can make a man a subject of any commonwealth, but his actually entering into it by positive engagement, and express promise and agreement.

* * * * *

Samuel Adams

Boston Gazette, October 14, 1771

The truth is, all might be free if they valued freedom, and defended it as they ought.

* * * * *

Alexander Hamilton

A Full Vindication December 15, 1774

The only distinction between freedom and slavery consists in this:

In the former state a man is governed by the laws to which he has given his consent, either in person or by his representative; in the latter, he is governed by the will of another. In the one case, his life and property are his own; in the other, they depend upon the pleasure of his master...

No reason can be assigned why one man should exercise any power or pre-eminence over his fellow-creatures more than another; unless they have voluntarily vested him with it. Since, then, Americans have not, by any act of theirs, empowered the British Parliament to make laws for them, it follows they can have no just authority to do it.

* * * * *

Samuel Adams
Boston Gazette, October 28, 1771
Every man being born free, says another distinguished writer, the son of a citizen, arrived at the years of discretion, may examine whether it be convenient for him to join in the society for which he was destined by birth.

If he finds that it will be no advantage for him to remain in it, he is at liberty to leave it, preserving as much as his new engagements will allow him, the love and gratitude he owes it.

* * * * *

Samuel Adams
The Rights Of The Colonists November 20, 1772
The natural liberty of man is to be free from any superior power on earth, and not to be under the will or legislative authority of man; but only to have the law of nature for his rule.

* * * * *

Samuel Adams
Letter to Ezra Whitmarsh April 13 1773
No greater Blessing can be desired by this Community than "Peace Prosperity & Happiness," and the Enjoyment of this Blessing depends upon civil & religious liberty.
* * * * *

Washington, concerned with the practicalities of maintaining liberty, points out that liberty cannot ultimately be separated from virtue. Liberty frees human life to grow and create, but if is taken no further than an excuse to act irresponsibly — with no productive ends — it cannot be maintained.

George Washington
Letter to John Augustine Washington, June 15, 1783
Liberty, when it degenerates into licentiousness, begets confusion, and frequently ends in Tyranny or some woeful catastrophe.

* * * * *

Washington reveals the goal that drove him to action: Civil and religious liberty.

George Washington
Letter to the Reformed German Congregation of New York City, November 27, 1783
The establishment of Civil and Religious Liberty was the Motive which induced me to the Field - the object is attained - and it now remains to be my earnest wish & prayer, that the Citizens of the United States could make a wise and virtuous use of the blessings placed before them.

* * * * *

Thomas Jefferson
Summary View of the Rights of British America, 1774
The God who gave us life, gave us liberty at the same time; the hand of force may destroy, but it cannot separate them.

* * * * *

Thomas Jefferson

Draft Constitution for Virginia June 1776

All persons shall have full and free liberty of religious opinion; nor shall any be compelled to attend or maintain any religious institution.

* * * * *

Thomas Jefferson

Letter to Isaac H. Tiffany 1819

Rightful liberty is unobstructed action according to our will within limits drawn around us by the equal rights of others.

I do not add "within the limits of the law" because law is often but the tyrant's will, and always so when it violates the rights of the individual.

* * * * *

Patrick Henry

Second Virginia Convention March 23, 1775

Is life so dear, or peace so sweet, as to be purchased at the price of chains and slavery? Forbid it, Almighty God!

I know not what course others may take; but as for me, give me liberty or give me death!

* * * * *

Samuel Adams

Boston Gazette, January 20, 1772

No free people, as the Pennsylvania Farmer has observed, ever existed, or ever can exist without, to use a common but strong expression, keeping the purse-strings in their hands.

* * * * *

Liberty, Suffering and Loss for

Samuel Adams
Letter to his wife November 7, 1775
We must be content to suffer the Loss of all things in this Life, rather than tamely surrender the public Liberty.

The Eyes of the People of Britain seem to be tightly closed; if they should ever be opened they will rejoice, and thank the Americans for resisting a Tyranny which is manifestly intended to overwhelm them and the whole British Empire.

Righteous Heaven will surely smile on a Cause so righteous as ours is, and our Country, if it does its Duty will see an End to its Oppressions.

Whether I shall live to rejoice with the Friends of Liberty and Virtue, my fellow Laborers in the Common Cause, is a Matter of no Consequence. I will endeavor by Gods Assistance, to act my little part well--to approve my self to Him, and trust every thing which concerns me to his all-gracious Providence.

* * * * *

Lies, Deception

George Washington
Letter to Dr. John Cochran, August 16, 1779
I hate deception, even where the imagination only is concerned.

* * * * *

Thomas Jefferson
Letter to Peter Carr August 19, 1785
He who permits himself to tell a lie once, finds it much easier to do it a second and third time, till at length it becomes habitual...

This falsehood of tongue leads to that of the heart, and in time depraves all its good dispositions.

* * * * *

Loss of Liberty

Samuel Adams

Boston Gazette, January 21, 1771

It is not effective to make the first attempt to enslave mankind by force: This strikes the imagination, and is alarming:

"Important changes happen imperceptibly: It is against silent & slow attacks that a nation ought to be particularly on its guard."

* * * * *

George Washington

Circular to the States, May 9, 1753

Arbitrary power is most easily established on the ruins of liberty abused to licentiousness.

* * * * *

James Madison

Speech at the Virginia Convention to ratify the Federal Constitution June 6, 1788

Since the general civilization of mankind, I believe there are more instances of the abridgment of the freedom of the people by gradual and silent encroachments of those in power, than by violent and sudden usurpations.

But, on a candid examination of history, we shall find that turbulence, violence, and abuse of power, by the majority trampling on the rights of the minority, have produced factions and commotions, which, in republics, have, more frequently than any other cause, produced despotism.

If we go over the whole history of ancient and modern republics, we shall find their destruction to have generally resulted from those causes.

* * * * *

James Madison
Letter to Thomas Jefferson May 13, 1798
Perhaps it is a universal truth that the loss of liberty at home is to be charged against provisions against danger, real or pretended, from abroad.

* * * * *

Samuel Adams
Boston Gazette, December 23, 1771
Remember my countrymen, it will be better to have your liberties ripped from you by force, than to have it said that you even implicitly surrendered them.

By "implicitly," Adams means surrendering rights without every saying so or admitting it.

* * * * *

James Madison

Thomas Jefferson
Quoted in The Republic of Letters: The Correspondence between Thomas Jefferson and James Madison
[On Madison] from three and thirty years' trial, I can say conscientiously that I do not know in the world a man of purer integrity, more dispassionate, disinterested, and devoted to republicanism; nor could I, in the whole scope of America and Europe, point out an abler head.

* * * * *

Majority Rule

James Madison
Letter to Thomas Jefferson October 17, 1788
Wherever the real power in a Government lies, there is the danger of oppression.

In our Governments, the real power lies in the majority of the community, and the invasion of private rights is chiefly to be seen, not from the acts of Government contrary to the sense of its constituents, but from acts in which the Government is the mere instrument of the major number of the constituents.

* * * * *

James Madison
Letter to James Monroe, October 5, 1786
There is no maxim in my opinion which is more liable to be misapplied, and which therefore needs clarification than the current one that the interest of the majority is the political standard of right and wrong...

In fact, it only reestablishes, under another name and a more deceptive form, force as the measure of right...

* * * * *

Making Decisions

Benjamin Franklin
Letter to Joseph Preistley September 19, 1772
When these difficult Cases occur, they are difficult chiefly because while we have them under Consideration all the Reasons pro and con are not present to the Mind at the same time; but sometimes one Set present themselves, and at other times another, the first being out of Sight. Hence the various

Purposes or Inclinations that alternately prevail, and the Uncertainty that perplexes us.

To get over this, my Way is, to divide half a Sheet of Paper by a Line into two Columns, writing over the one Pro, and over the other Con. Then during three or four Days Consideration I put down under the different Heads short Hints of the different Motives that at different Times occur to me for or against the Measure. When I have thus got them all together in one View, I endeavor to estimate their respective Weights; and where I find two, one on each side, that seem equal, I strike them both out: If I find a Reason pro equal to some two Reasons con, I strike out the three. If I judge some two Reasons con equal to some three Reasons pro, I strike out the five; and thus proceeding I find at length where the Balance lies; and if after a Day or two of farther Consideration nothing new that is of Importance occurs on either side, I come to a Determination accordingly.

And though the Weight of Reasons cannot be taken with the Precision of Algebraic Quantities, yet when each is thus considered separately and comparatively, and the whole lies before me, I think I can judge better, and am less likely to take a rash Step; and in fact I have found great Advantage from this kind of Equation, in what may be called Moral or Prudential Algebra.

* * * * *

Man

Thomas Jefferson
Letter to Jean Nicholas Demeunier January 24, 1786
What a stupendous, what an incomprehensible machine is man! Who can endure toil, famine, stripes, imprisonment and death itself in vindication of his own liberty, and the next moment... inflict on his fellow men a bondage, one hour of which is fraught with more misery than ages of that which he rose in rebellion to oppose.

Marriage

Jokes about marriage were as popular in Franklin's day as in our own; and Franklin liked jokes. Nonetheless, he maintains here that marriage is the best state for people.

Benjamin Franklin
Letter to John Sargent, January 27, 1783
The married state is, after all our jokes, the happiest, being conformable to our natures. Man and woman have each of them qualities and tempers in which the other is deficient and which in union contribute to the common felicity. Single and separate, they are not the complete human being; they are like the odd halves of scissors; they cannot answer the end of their formation.

* * * * *

Merit

George Washington
Address to the Officers of the Virginia Regiment, January 8, 1756
I shall make it the most agreeable part of my duty to study merit, and reward the brave and deserving.

* * * * *

George Washington
Letter to Nicholas Pike, June 20, 1786
In my opinion, every effort of genius, and all attempts towards improving useful knowledge ought to meet with encouragement in this country.

* * * * *

Samuel Adams

Letter to Elbridge Geary September 16, 1775

There are many military geniuses at present unemployed and overlooked...

They must be sought after, for modest merit declines pushing itself into public view.

* * * * *

The Militia

The citizen militia was a military strategy used by the American colonies and in the early days of the United States. Military weapons and tactics have changed repetitively since that time, and the militia is no longer generally used, but it remains a valid strategy and may (or may not) be found preferable in the future.

Samuel Adams

Letter to Elbridge Gerry October 29, 1775

Your militia is your natural strength, which ought under your own direction to be employed for your own safety and protection.

It is a misfortune to a colony to become the seat of war. It is always dangerous to the liberties of the people to have an army stationed among them, over which they have no control. There is at present a necessity for it; the continental army is kept up within our colony, most evidently for our immediate security. But it should be remembered that history affords abundant instances of established armies making themselves the masters of those countries, which they were designed to protect.

There may be no danger of this at present, but it should be a caution not to trust the whole military strength of a colony in the hands of commanders independent of its established legislature.

* * * * *

George Mason

June 14, 1788, quoted in The Debates in the Several State Conventions on the Adoption of the Federal Constitution, 1861
Forty years ago, when the resolution of enslaving America was formed in Great Britain, the British Parliament was advise by an artful man, who was governor of Pennsylvania, to disarm the people; that it was the best and most effectual was to enslave them; but that they should not do it openly, but weaken them, and let them sink gradually, by totally disusing and neglecting the militia.

* * * * *

Thomas Jefferson

Inaugural Address March 4, 1801
A well-disciplined militia, our best reliance in peace and for the first moments of war till regulars may relieve them.

* * * * *

George Washington

Letter to the president of Congress September 24, 1776
To place any dependence upon militia, is, assuredly, resting upon a broken staff.

Men just dragged from the tender scenes of domestic life - unaccustomed to the din of arms - totally unacquainted with every kind of military skill, which being followed by a lack of confidence in themselves when opposed to troops regularly trained, disciplined, and appointed, superior in knowledge, and superior in arms, makes them timid and ready to fly from their own shadows.

* * * * *

George Mason

Virginia Declaration of Rights 1776
That a well regulated militia, composed of the body of the people, trained to arms, is the proper, natural, and safe defense of a free state.

That standing armies, in time of peace, should be avoided as dangerous to liberty; and that, in all cases, the military should be under strict subordination to, and be governed by, the civil power.

* * * * *

Miracles

Benjamin Franklin
Letter to Abbé Morellet 1779

We hear of the conversion of water into wine at the marriage in Cana as of a miracle. But this conversion is, through the goodness of God, made every day before our eyes.

Behold the rain which descends from heaven upon our vineyards; there it enters the roots of the vines, to be changed into wine; a constant proof that God loves us, and loves to see us happy.

The miracle in question was only performed to hasten the operation, under circumstances of present necessity, which required it.

* * * * *

Mistakes

Samuel Adams
Independent Chronicle, January 20, 1794

Honest men will not feel themselves disgusted, when mistakes are pointed out to them with decency, candor and friendship, nor will they, when convinced of truth, think their own dignity degraded by correcting their own errors.

* * * * *

George Washington

Farewell Address September 17, 1796

Though, in reviewing the incidents of my administration, I am unconscious of intentional error, I am nevertheless too sensible of my defects not to think it probable that I may have committed many errors.

Whatever they may be, I fervently beseech the Almighty to avert or mitigate the evils toward which they may tend.

I shall also carry with me the hope, that my Country will never cease to view them with indulgence; and that, after forty-five years of my life dedicated to its service with an upright zeal, the faults of incompetent abilities will be consigned to oblivion, as myself must soon be to the mansions of rest.

* * * * *

Benjamin Franklin

Poor Richard's Almanac

How few there are who have courage enough to own their faults, or resolution enough to mend them!

* * * * *

Mistreatment

George Washington

Letter to Joseph Jones, March 18, 1783

Nothing is too extravagant to expect from men who conceive they are ungratefully and unjustly dealt by.

* * * * *

Money, Ignorance Regarding

John Adams
Letter to Thomas Jefferson August 23, 1787
All the perplexities, confusions, and distresses in America arise, not from defects in their constitution or confederation, not from a want of honor or virtue, so much as from downright ignorance of the nature of coin, credit, and circulation.

* * * * *

Names

Here Franklin points out an important fact: That knowing the name of something (as is too often the primary goal of schooling) is wholly separate from understanding the nature of the thing.

Benjamin Franklin
Poor Richard's Almanac
What signifies knowing the Names, if you know not the Natures of Things.

* * * * *

The New Testament

Among most of the founders, the New Testament was clearly considered a Holy book; so much so that they had no reason to comment upon it – its value was universally known. Jefferson the philosopher, however, differs, and has very specific opinions on the authenticity of the New Testament:

Thomas Jefferson
Letter to John Adams January 24, 1814
In the New Testament there is internal evidence that parts of it have proceeded from an extraordinary man; and that other parts are of the fabric of very inferior minds. It is as easy to separate those parts, as to pick out diamonds from dunghills.

* * * * *

Obedience

Here, as often, Sam Adams is the enemy of obedience.

Samuel Adams
Boston Gazette, November 11, 1771
Even in these enlightened times, the people in some parts of the world are so bewitched by the enchantments of priest-craft and king-craft, as to believe that though they sin against their own consciences, in compliance with the instruction of the one, or in obedience to the command of the other, they shall never suffer, but shall be rewarded in the world to come, for being so implicitly subject to the higher powers.

* * * * *

Observation & Proof

Among many other things, Benjamin Franklin was a scientist. This passage on proofs was written with the great French Scientist Lavoisier, who proved the conservation of mass, discovered oxygen and hydrogen, and made many other contributions.

Benjamin Franklin and Antoine Lavoisier
Rapport des commissaires chargés par le roi de l'examen du magnétisme animal 1784

The art of concluding from experience and observation consists in evaluating probabilities, in estimating if they are high or numerous enough to constitute proof.

This type of calculation is more complicated and more difficult than one might think. It demands a great discernment, generally above the power of common people.

The success of charlatans, sorcerers, and alchemists — and all those who abuse public credulity — is founded on errors in this type of calculation.

* * * * *

Offense

Franklin opines that if he had to pay attention to everyone who claims to be offended, he'd never get much done.

Benjamin Franklin

If all printers were determined not to print anything till they were sure it would offend nobody, there would be very little printed.

* * * * *

Old Age

Samuel Adams
Letter to John Adams March 9, 1779
Even old Age which is making Strides towards me shall not prevail to make me grumpy.

I find that an older Man than I am, can in the apparent Coolness of Mind, stab a dreaded Rival to the Vitals. His Words are like Honey, but there is a large Mixture of Poison.

You who are in the Midst of Life & Usefulness, do not expect to escape the envenomed Shaft, but you have always the Cure at hand: Moderation, Fortitude & Prudence.

It matters little what becomes of an old worn out Servant in this World. He has his foot on the Grave & with Pleasure views it.

But the virtuous Patriot, who is in the full Exercise of the Powers of Body & Mind, shall have my remaining feeble Voice in his Support against the insidious Enemy of himself & Mankind.

* * * * *

Jefferson, upon assuming the Presidency, sought the advice of Sam Adams. The elderly Adams writes back:

Samuel Adams
Letter to Thomas Jefferson April 24, 1801
Be assured, that my esteem for you is as cordial, if possible, as yours is to me. Though an Old Man cannot advise you, he can give you his Blessing. You have devoutly my Blessing and my Prayers.

* * * * *

Thomas Jefferson
Letter to Charles Willson Peale August 20, 1811
But though an old man, I am but a young gardener.

* * * * *

Over-Population

In an unusual passage, James Madison expresses his opinions on over-population and its dangers.

James Madison
Population and Emigration National Gazette November 21, 1791
Man who preys both on the vegetable and animal species, is himself a prey to neither. He too possesses the reproductive principle far beyond the degree requisite for the bare continuance of his species. What becomes of the surplus of human life to which this principle is competent?

It is either, 1st destroyed by infanticide, as among the Chinese and Spartans; or 2nd, it is stifled or starved, as among other nations whose population is commensurate to its food; or 3rd, it is consumed by wars and endemic diseases; or 4th, it overflows, by emigration, to places where a surplus of food is attainable.

* * * * *

Paper Money

Thomas Jefferson
Letter to Edward Carrington May 27, 1788
Paper is poverty... it is only the ghost of money, and not money itself.

* * * * *

Samuel Adams

Letter to Samuel Cooper November 7, 1780

Had our Money been stable we might have contracted for the Supply of our Army; but the Paper, as all the World knows, is depreciated, for which we are in part obliged to our Enemies, who are dexterous in counterfeiting.

* * * * *

Parties

The administration of George Washington (that is, the first eight years of the United States government) and the first few sessions of the US Congress were nonpartisan. Legislators came to their meetings and decided their vote upon the merits of the bills presented to them. They dealt with the issues directly.

Once parties became involved, however, a new layer came into play. The legislator now had to consider whether the party would approve or disapprove of his votes. His attention was drawn away from the actual merits of the bill and away from his constituents.

The appeal of parties to voters was that they could pool their power to vote candidates into office and thus gain a much greater grip on the government. This, if we are to be honest, meant that they could force others to do the things that they wanted. (Government is force, and not persuasion.)

The adoption of political parties diminished cooperation and made force a larger component of American life. Most of the founders strongly opposed parties, as this section illustrates.

It is sadly ironic that a primary argument for a strong central government (in the Federalist papers) was that it would prevent factional fighting. Our first quote illustrates this:

James Madison

Federalist #10

Among the numerous advantages promised by a well constructed Union, none deserves to be more accurately developed than its tendency to break and control the violence of faction. The friend of popular governments never finds himself so much alarmed for their character and fate, as when he contemplates their propensity to this dangerous vice. He will not fail, therefore, to set a due value on any plan which, without violating the principles to which he is attached, provides a proper cure for it.

Federalist 14 says, very explicitly: "the necessity of the Union, as... the proper antidote for the diseases of faction."

* * * * *

Samuel Adams
Boston Gazette, December 16, 1771
I am no party man, unless a firm attachment to the cause of Liberty and Truth will denominate one such.

* * * * *

Thomas Jefferson
Letter to Francis Hopkinson March 13, 1789
I never submitted the whole system of my opinions to the creed of any party of men whatever in religion, in philosophy, in politics, or in anything else where I was capable of thinking for myself. Such an addiction is the last degradation of a free and moral agent. If I could not go to heaven but with a party, I would not go there at all.

This quote contradicts the assertions of some that he was founding the Democratic-Republican party at about this time.

* * * * *

John Adams
Letter to Jonathan Jackson October 2, 1789
There is nothing which I dread so much as a division of the republic into two great parties, each arranged under its leader, and concerting measures in opposition to each other. This, in

my humble apprehension, is to be dreaded as the greatest political evil under our Constitution.

* * * * *

George Washington
Farewell Address September 17, 1796
One of the expedients of party to acquire influence within particular districts is to misrepresent the opinions and aims of other districts. You cannot shield yourselves too much against the jealousies and heartburnings which spring from these misrepresentations; they tend to render alien to each other those who ought to be bound together by fraternal affection.

* * * * *

George Washington
Farewell Address September 17, 1796
All obstructions to the execution of the laws, all combinations and associations, under whatever plausible character, with the real design to direct, control, counteract, or awe the regular deliberation and action of the constituted authorities, are destructive of this fundamental principle and of fatal tendency. They serve to organize faction; to give it an artificial and extraordinary force; to put in the place of the delegated will of the nation the will of a party, often a small but artful and enterprising minority of the community, and, according to the alternate triumphs of different parties, to make the public administration the mirror of the ill-concerted and incongruous projects of faction rather than the organ of consistent and wholesome plans, digested by common counsels and modified by mutual interests.

However combinations or associations of the above description may now and then address popular ends, they are likely, in the course of time and events, to become potent engines by which cunning, ambitious, and unprincipled men will be enabled to subvert the power of the people, and to usurp for themselves the reins of government.

George Washington

Farewell Address September 17, 1796

This spirit [of party], unfortunately, is inseparable from our nature, having its root in the strongest passions of the human mind. It exists under different shapes in all governments, more or less stifled, controlled, or repressed; but in those of the popular form it is seen in its greatest rankness and is truly their worst enemy...

It serves always to distract the public councils and enfeeble the public administration. It agitates the community with ill-founded jealousies and false alarms; kindles the animosity of one part against another; foments occasional riot and insurrection. It opens the door to foreign influence and corruption, which find a facilitated access to the government itself through the channels of party passion.

* * * * *

Patience

Samuel Adams

Letter to Joseph Hawley April 15 1776

Let us not be impatient. It requires Time to convince the doubting and inspire the timid.

* * * * *

Thomas Jefferson

Letter to John Taylor June 1798 (following passage of the Alien and Sedition Acts)

A little patience, and we shall see the reign of witches pass over, their spells dissolve, and the people, recovering their true sight, restore their government to its true principles.

It is true that in the meantime we are suffering deeply in spirit, and incurring the horrors of a war and long oppressions of enormous public debt.

If the game runs sometimes against us at home we must have patience till luck turns, and then we shall have an opportunity of winning back the principles we have lost, for this is a game where principles are at stake.

Jefferson won the Presidency two years after and was able to reverse most of the things he and Taylor were discussing.

* * * * *

Patriotism

The problem with patriotism and patriot acts is to define them. Following national leaders without analysis or question is not really patriotism. (Other wise we wouldn't blame Nazis for following the worst of Hitler's orders.) So, what exactly is patriotism? Here, Samuel Adams and George Washington give examples:

Samuel Adams
Boston Gazette, June 12, 1780
Formerly this great contest [of separation from Britain] was carried on upon paper. The conspirators against the rights and liberties of our country left no art untried, to induce the people to submit to their unrighteous claims. But they were circumvented by our watchful patriots.

They were, if I may use the expression, out-reasoned by some, and laughed off the stage by others; and we will never forget those steadfast and persevering friends, who forever proved themselves incapable of being bribed by the soft whispers of flattery, or awed by foul-mouthed calumny and the threats of power.

Afterwards the contest became more serious and important. The people of this country were not driven to take up arms, they did it voluntarily in defense of their liberty.

They properly considered themselves as called by God, and warranted by Him, to encounter every hazard in the common cause of Man.

* * * * *

Samuel Adams
Letter to James Warren October 24, 1780
If ever the Time should come, when vain & aspiring Men shall possess the highest Seats in Government, our Country will stand in Need of its experienced Patriots to prevent its Ruin.

* * * * *

George Washington
Encouraging his men to re-enlist in the army December 31, 1776
My brave fellows, you have done all I asked you to do, and more than can be reasonably expected; but your country is at stake, your wives, your houses and all that you hold dear.

You have worn yourselves out with fatigues and hardships, but we do not know how to spare you. If you will consent to stay one month longer, you will render a service to the cause of liberty, and to your country, which you probably can never do under any other circumstances.

* * * * *

Washington, as shown here, is not overly fond patriotism itself:

George Washington
Letter to John Banister, April 21, 1778
I do not mean to exclude altogether the ideas of patriotism. I know it exists, and I know it has done much in the present contest. But I will venture to assert, that a great and lasting war can never be supported on this principle alone. It must be aided by a prospect of interest or some reward.

For a time, patriotism may, of itself, push men to action: to bear much, to encounter difficulties; but it will not endure unassisted by interest.

* * * * *

Peace

George Washington
Letter to Elbridge Gerry, January 29, 1780
There is nothing so likely to produce peace as to be well prepared to meet an enemy.

* * * * *

Washington here repeats an ancient and true theme. But this comment also implies that all or most states are predators by nature: that they will attack if they are able to attack. History illustrates this in abundance, but it remains an unpleasant thought to most people.

George Washington
Address to both Houses of Congress January 8, 1790
To be prepared for war is one of the most effectual means of preserving peace.

* * * * *

The People

Jefferson believes that the only safe place for power is in the people, but he also acknowledges that the people may do stupid things. Even so, he says, the answer is not to move power away from the people, but to better inform them.

Thomas Jefferson
Letter to William Charles Jarvis September 28, 1820
I know no safe depository of the ultimate powers of the society but the people themselves; and if we think them not enlightened enough to exercise their control with wholesome discretion, the remedy is not to take it from them, but to inform their discretion by education.

This is the true corrective of abuses of constitutional power.

* * * * *

Philosophy

Philosophic thoughts from Thomas Jefferson, John Adams and Alexander Hamilton:

Thomas Jefferson
Letter to Thomas Law June 13, 1814
If we did a good act merely from love of God and a belief that it is pleasing to Him, where does the morality of the Atheist come from? ... Their virtue, then, must have had some other foundation than the love of God.

* * * * *

Thomas Jefferson
Letter to John Adams July 5, 1814
The Christian priesthood, finding the doctrines of Christ levelled to every understanding, and too plain to need

explanation, saw in the mysticism of Plato, materials with which they might build up an artificial system, which might, from its indistinctness, admit everlasting controversy, give employment for their order, and introduce it to profit, power and pre-eminence.

The doctrines which flowed from the lips of Jesus himself are within the comprehension of a child ; but thousands of volumes have not yet explained the Platonisms engrafted on them; and for this obvious reason, that nonsense can never be explained.

* * * * *

Thomas Jefferson
Letter to John Adams 1816
I believe... that every human mind feels pleasure in doing good to another.

* * * * *

Thomas Jefferson
Letter to William Short October 31, 1819
As you say of yourself, I too am an Epicurian. I consider the genuine (not the imputed) doctrines of Epicurus as containing everything rational in moral philosophy which Greece and Rome have left us.

* * * * *

John Adams
Letter to John Taylor April 15, 1814
Liberty, according to my metaphysics, is an intellectual quality, an attribute that belongs not to fate nor to chance. Neither possesses it, neither is capable of it. There is nothing moral or immoral in the idea of it.

The definition of it is a self-determining power in an intellectual agent. It implies thought and choice and power; it can choose between objects, indifferent in point of morality, neither morally good nor morally evil.

* * * * *

Alexander Hamilton
Letter April 16, 1802
Men are rather reasoning than reasonable animals, for the most part governed by the impulse of passion.

* * * * *

The Poor

Benjamin Franklin
Relating to prices and the poor 1766
I am for doing good to the poor, but I differ in opinion of the methods.

I think the best way of doing good to the poor, is not making them comfortable in poverty, but leading or driving them out of it.

In my youth I traveled much, and I observed in different countries, that the more public provisions were made for the poor, the less they provided for themselves, and of course became poorer. And, on the contrary, the less was done for them, the more they did for themselves, and became richer.

* * * * *

Benjamin Franklin
On the Price of Corn and Management of the Poor November 29, 1766
I think the best way of doing good to the poor, is not making them easy in poverty, but leading or driving them out of it.

* * * * *

Franklin is very clear: No one should be ashamed of having been poor.

Benjamin Franklin
Poor Richard's Almanac
Having been poor is no shame, but being ashamed of it is.

* * * * *

Popularity

Samuel Adams
Boston Gazette, April 2, 1781
The raging Thirst for popular Applause, a Disease with which little minds are usually tormented.

* * * * *

John Adams
Personal Diary February 19, 1756
No man is entirely free from weakness and imperfection in this life. Men of the most exalted genius and active minds are generally most perfect slaves to the love of fame.

They sometimes descend to dirty tricks and schemes in pursuit of honor or reputation, like the miser does in pursuit of gold.

* * * * *

Power

Samuel Adams
Boston Gazette, January 21, 1771
Power, especially in times of corruption, makes men wanton; so that it intoxicates the mind.

Unless those entrusted with power are carefully watched, such is the weakness or the perverseness of human nature, that they will be apt to domineer over the people, instead of governing them.

"Wanton" means unrestrained, loose, and without care for what is right.

* * * * *

James Madison
Speech at the Constitutional Convention, July 11, 1787
All men having power ought to be distrusted to a certain degree.

* * * * *

John Adams
Letter to Thomas Jefferson February 2, 1815
Power always sincerely, conscientiously, de très bon foi, believes itself right.

Power always thinks it has a great soul and vast views, beyond the comprehension of the weak.

* * * * *

Power & Tyranny

George Mason
Virginia Declaration of Rights 1776
All power is vested in, and consequently derived from, the people. Magistrates are their trustees and servants, and at all times answerable to them.

* * * * *

Samuel Adams

Boston Gazette, November 25, 1771

Did not our ancestors, when they accepted this Charter, understand that they had contracted for a free government? And did not the King on his part intend that it should be so?

Was it not understood, that by this contract, every power of government was to be under a check adequate to the importance of it, without which, according to the best reasoners on government, and the experience of mankind in all ages of the world, that power must be a tyranny?

* * * * *

Samuel Adams

Letter to James Warren October 24, 1780

If ever the Time should come, when vain & aspiring Men shall possess the highest Seats in Government, our Country will stand in Need of its experienced Patriots to prevent its Ruin.

There may be more Danger of this, than some, even of our well disposed Citizens may imagine... Power is intoxicating; and Men legally vested with it too often discover a Disposition to make an ill Use of it & an Unwillingness to part with it.

* * * * *

Samuel Adams

Letter to Elbridge Gerry April 23, 1784

There is a Degree of Watchfulness over all Men possessed of Power or Influence upon which the Liberties of Mankind much depend.

It is necessary to guard against the Infirmities of the best as well as the Wickedness of the worst of Men.

Such is the Weakness of human Nature that Tyranny has oftener sprang from that than any other Source. It is this that unravels the Mystery of Millions being enslaved by a few.

John Adams

Notes for an oration at Braintree Spring 1772

There is danger from all men. The only maxim of a free government ought to be to trust no man living with power to endanger the public liberty.

* * * * *

John Adams

Novanglus Papers Boston Gazette 1774-1775

"Nip the shoots of arbitrary power in the bud," is the only maxim which can ever preserve the liberties of any people.

* * * * *

Power-Seekers

Samuel Adams

Letter to Elbridge Gerry October 29, 1775

I hope the utmost caution will be used in the choice of men for public officers.

It is to be expected that some who are void of the least regard to the public, will put on the appearance and even speak boldly the language of patriots, with the sole purpose of gaining the confidence of the public, and securing the loaves and fishes for themselves or their sons or other connections.

Men who stand candidates for public posts, should be critically traced in their views and pretensions, and though we would despise mean and base suspicions, there is a degree of jealousy which is absolutely necessary in this degenerate state of mankind, and is indeed at all times to be considered as a political virtue.

* * * * *

Thomas Jefferson

Letter to Henry Lee August 10, 1824

Men by their constitutions are naturally divided into two parties:

1. Those who fear and distrust the people, and wish to draw all powers from them into the hands of the higher classes.

2. Those who identify themselves with the people, have confidence in them, cherish and consider them as the most honest and safe, although not the most wise depositary of the public interests.

In every country these two parties exist, and in every one where they are free to think, speak, and write, they will declare themselves. Call them, therefore, liberals and serviles, Jacobins and Ultras, whigs and tories, republicans and federalists, aristocrats and democrats, or by whatever name you please, they are the same parties still and pursue the same object.

The ultimate names aristocrats and democrats are the true ones, expressing the essence of all.

* * * * *

Prayer

Public Days of Prayer were common during the Revolution. Sam Adams in particular was involved with many of them, as were many others. Prayer was almost universally held in high regard. Here, however, Franklin looks at a different aspect of the situation:

Benjamin Franklin

Poor Richard's Almanac

Serving God is Doing Good to Man, but Praying is thought an easier Service, and therefore more generally chosen.

* * * * *

Preparation For Conflict

As mentioned previously, talking bravely is a far different thing that stepping into danger. Here we see the founders doing the harder thing.

This first quote is written as Washington is about to be appointed to head the Continental Army and to face the fearsome British Army.

George Washington
Diary Entry, June 1, 1774
Went to church and fasted all day.

* * * * *

This was written two days after accepting his appointment to head the Continental Army. Washington is evidently planning for his family and farm after his (quite possible) death.

George Washington
Letter to Martha Washington, June 18, 1775
Life is always uncertain, and common prudence dictates to every man the necessity of settling his earthly affairs, while it is in his power, and while the mind is calm and undisturbed.

* * * * *

Samuel Adams
Letter to Stephan Collins January 31, 1775
Our "worthy citizen" Mr Paul Revere will explain to you the intelligence which we have just received from England. It puts me in mind of what I remember to have heard you observe, that we may all be soon under the necessity of keeping shooting irons. God grant that we may not be brought to extremity or otherwise prepare us for all events.

* * * * *

Samuel Adams

Letter to Arthur Lee January 29, 1775

The People are universally disposed to wait till they can hear what Effect the Applications of the Continental Congress will have, in hopes that the new Parliament will reverse the Laws & measures of the old, abolish that System of Tyranny which was planed in 1763 (perhaps before), confirm the just Rights of the Colonies and restore Harmony to the British Empire. God grant they may not be disappointed!

In case they are disappointed, they have been, & are still, exercising themselves in military Discipline and providing the necessary Means of Defense.

I am well informed that in every Part of the Province there are selected Numbers of Men, called Minute Men--that they are well disciplined & well provided--and that upon a very short Notice they will be able to assemble a formidable Army.

They are resolved however not to be the Aggressors in an open Quarrel with the [British] Troops; but animated with an unquenchable Love of Liberty they will support their righteous Claim to it, to the utmost Extremity.

They are filled with Indignation to hear that Hutchinson & their other inveterate Enemies have hinted to the Nation that they are Cowards… but whenever it is brought to the Test it will be found to be a fatal Delusion.

The People are recollecting the Achievements of their Ancestors and whenever it shall be necessary for them to draw their Swords in the Defense of their Liberties, they will show themselves to be worthy of such Ancestors.

* * * * *

Washington will be comforted, even in defeat, if he provides his best effort.

George Washington
Letter to Col. Burwell Bassett, June 19, 1775
I shall not be deprived... of a comfort in the worst event, if I retain a consciousness of having acted to the best of my judgment.

* * * * *

George Washington
Letter to Col. Burwell Bassett, his brother-in-law, June 19, 1775
I have been called upon by the unanimous voice of the Colonies to the command of the Continental Army. It is an honor I by no means aspired to.

It is an honor I wished to avoid, not only from an unwillingness to quit the peaceful enjoyment of my Family, but because I am convinced of my own inability & lack of experience in the conduct of so momentous a concern.

But the fondness of the Congress, added to some political motives, left me without a choice.

May God grant, therefore, that my acceptance of it may be attended with some good to the common cause, & without injury (from lack of knowledge) to my own reputation.

I can answer with three things: a firm belief of the justice of our cause, close attention in the pursuit of it, and the strictest integrity. If these cannot compensate for ability & experience, the cause will suffer, & more than probable my character along with it, as reputation derives its principal support from success.

* * * * *

George Washington
Letter to Augustine Washington, June 20, 1775
I shall hope that my friends will visit and endeavor to keep up the spirits of my wife, as much as they can, as my departure will, I know, be a cutting stroke upon her.

* * * * *

Patrick Henry
Second Virginia Convention March 23, 1775
Sir, we are not weak if we make a proper use of those means which the God of nature hath placed in our power…

The battle, sir, is not to the strong alone; it is to the vigilant, the active, the brave.

* * * * *

The Presidency

John Adams
Letter to Josiah Quincy III February 14, 1825
No man who ever held the office of president would congratulate a friend on obtaining it. He will make one man ungrateful, and a hundred men his enemies, for every position he can bestow.

* * * * *

George Washington
Comment to General Henry Knox before assuming office March 1789
My movements to the chair of Government will be accompanied by feelings not unlike those of a culprit who is going to the place of his execution

I am so unwilling, in the evening of a life nearly consumed in public cares, to quit a peaceful home for an Ocean of difficulties, without the political skill, abilities and inclination which is necessary to manage the helm.

Priests

Thomas Jefferson
Letter to Mrs. Harrison Smith August 6, 1816

It is in our lives, and not from our words, that our religion must be read. By the same test the world must judge me.

But this does not satisfy the priesthood. They must have a positive, a declared assent to all their interested absurdities.

My opinion is that there would never have been an infidel, if there had never been a priest.

* * * * *

John Adams
Letter to John Taylor 1814

The priesthood have, in all ancient nations, nearly monopolized learning.

Read over again all the accounts we have of Hindoos, Chaldeans, Persians, Greeks, Romans, Celts, Teutons: We shall find that priests had all the knowledge, and really governed mankind.

Examine Mahometanism, trace Christianity from its first promulgation; knowledge has been almost exclusively confined to the clergy.

And, even since the Reformation, when or where has existed a Protestant or dissenting sect who would tolerate A Free Inquiry?

The blackest vulgarity, most ungentlemanly insolence, the most yahooish brutality is patiently endured, accepted, propagated and applauded, but touch a solemn truth in collision with a dogma of a sect, and even though capable of the clearest proof, and you will soon find you have disturbed a nest, and the hornets will swarm about your legs and hands, and fly into your face and eyes.

* * * * *

Priests and Lawyers

Jefferson (who was a lawyer) doesn't go quite so far as to call lawyers a new class of priests, but he draws a parallel.

Thomas Jefferson
Letter to Horatio G. Spafford March 17, 1814

In every country and in every age, the priest has been hostile to liberty. He is always in alliance with the despot, abetting his abuses in return for the protection of his own…

They have perverted the best religion ever preached to man into mystery and jargon, unintelligible to all mankind, and therefore the safer engine for their purposes.

With the lawyers it is a new thing. They have, in the mother country, been generally the prime supporters of the free principles of their constitution. But there, too, they have changed.

* * * * *

Principles

Thomas Jefferson
Letter to Samuel Kercheval 1816

Lay down true principles and adhere to them inflexibly. Do not be frightened into their surrender by the alarms of the timid, or the croakings of wealth against the ascendance of the people.

George Mason
Virginia Declaration of Rights 1776

No free government, or the blessings of liberty, can be preserved to any people but by a firm adherence to justice, moderation, temperance, frugality, and virtue and by frequent recurrence to fundamental principles.

* * * * *

Privacy, Secrecy

Samuel Adams
Letter to John Adams April 16, 1784
It is often inconvenient, perhaps unsafe, to trust ones Confidential Letters to indiscrete, however honest, Friends. Detached Parts of them being given out, they may be made to bear a different Construction from what was intended, and answer the Purpose of interested & designing Men.

* * * * *

Samuel Adams
Letter to an unknown recipient, January 10, 1778
I may explain my self more fully in another Letter. Adieu my friend. Burn this.

* * * * *

George Washington
Letter to Major Henry Lee October 20, 1780
The most inviolable secrecy must be observed on all hands.

* * * * *

Property

Samuel Adams
Letter to Benjamin Franklin, June 29, 1771
The charter of this province recognizes the natural Right of all men to dispose of their property.

* * * * *

Samuel Adams
Boston Gazette, September 9, 1771

The supreme power says Mr. Locke, is not, nor can possibly be absolutely arbitrary, over the lives and fortunes of the people.

The supreme power cannot take from any man any part of his property without his own consent. The preservation of property being the end of government, and that for which men enter into society; it necessarily supposes and requires that the people should have property, without which they must be supposed to lose that by entering into society, which was the end for which they entered into it.

Men therefore in society having property, they have such a right to the goods which by the law of the community are theirs, that no body hath a right to take their substance or any part of it from them without their consent. Without this, they have no property at all.

Note that Adams uses "society" in the older way: Society, the voluntary state of association among individuals, and not "A society," a giant group with a mandatory set of rules.

* * * * *

Samuel Adams
Boston Gazette, December 23, 1771

Mr. Locke has often been quoted in the present dispute between Britain and her colonies, and very much to our purpose. His reasoning is so forceful that no one has even attempted to disprove it.

He holds that:

"The preservation of property is the end [purpose or goal] of government, and that for which men enter into society.

"It therefore necessarily supposes and requires that the people should have property, and not that they should lose it by entering into society, since that was the end for which they entered into society. That would be too absurdity for any man to claim.

"Therefore men in society having property have a right to the goods, which by the law of the community are theirs, that no person has the right to take any part of their property without their consent:

"Without this, they could have no property at all. For I truly can have no property in that which another rightfully take from me when he pleases, against my consent.

"Therefore, it is a mistake to think that the supreme power of any commonwealth can dispose of the estates of the subjects arbitrarily, or take any part of them at its pleasure. The prince or senate can never have a power to take to themselves the whole or any part of the subjects property without their own consent; for this would be in effect to have no property at all."

This is the reasoning of that great and good man.

* * * * *

Samuel Adams
Boston Gazette, December 23, 1771
That sage of the law, Lord Camden, declared in his speech upon the declaratory bill, that:

"Taxation and representation are inseparably united: This position is founded on the laws of nature: It is more: It is itself an eternal law of nature

"Whatever is a man's own is absolutely his own; and no man has a right to take it from him without his consent, either expressed by himself or his representative.

Whoever attempts to do it, attempts an injury: Whoever does it, commits a robbery: He throws down the distinction between liberty and slavery."

* * * * *

John Adams
Defense of the Constitutions of Government 1787

The moment the idea is admitted into society, that property is not as sacred as the law of God, and that there is not a force of law and public justice to protect it, anarchy and tyranny commence.

If "Thou shall not covet," and "Thou shall not steal," are not commandments of Heaven, they must be made inviolable precepts in every society, before it can be civilized or made free.

* * * * *

Providence In The War

George Washington
Letter to Reed, during the siege of Boston January 14, 1776

I have often thought how much happier I should have been, if instead of accepting of a command under such circumstances, I had taken my musket upon my shoulders and entered the rank, or if I could have justified the measure of posterity, and my own conscience, had retired to the back country, and lived in a wigwam.

If I shall be able to rise superior to these, and many other difficulties which might be enumerated, I shall most religiously believe that the finger of Providence is in it, to blind the eyes of our enemies; for surely if we get well through this month, it must be for lack of them knowing the disadvantages we labor under.

Could I have foreseen the difficulties which have come upon us, could I have known that such a backwardness would have been discovered in the old soldiers to the service, all the generals upon earth should not have convinced me of the propriety of delaying an attack upon Boston till this time.

* * * * *

The Public

Samuel Adams
Letter to Arthur Lee, April 19 1771

Perhaps there never was a time when the political Affairs of America were in a more dangerous State.

Such is the numbness of Men in general, and their neglect of things of real importance, that steady and active perseverance on the difficult path of Virtue (from which trivial things may suffer) is barely to be expected.

The majority are necessarily engaged in private affairs for the support of their own families. When, at a fortunate moment the public awakens to a sense of danger, and a manly resentment is kindled, it is difficult for so many separate communities (as there are in all the Colonies), to agree in one consistent plan of Opposition.

Meanwhile, those who serve as instruments of Oppression have all the necessary resources for appealing to the passions of Men: Using the Necessities of some, the Vanity of others, and the Timidity of all.

* * * * *

Samuel Adams
Boston Gazette, October 7, 1771

In all ages the arrogant part of the clergy have adored the Great Man, and shown a thorough contempt for the understanding of the people.

* * * * *

Samuel Adams
Boston Gazette, October 14, 1771

Our enemies would love for us to lie down on the bed of sloth and security, and persuade ourselves that there is no danger.

They are daily administering this opiate with multiplied arts and fantasies, and I am sorry to observe that the gilded pill is alluring to some who call themselves the friends of Liberty.

"Sloth" is laziness. "Gilded" means gold-covered.

* * * * *

Public Credit

By "Public Credit" Washington means the ability of the government to borrow money at necessary moments – that it be known as a good credit risk

George Washington
Farewell Address September 17, 1796
As a very important source of strength and security, cherish public credit.

One method of preserving it is, to use it as sparingly as possible; avoiding occasions of expense by cultivating peace, but remembering also that timely disbursements to prepare for danger frequently prevent much greater disbursements to repel it; avoiding likewise the accumulation of debt, not only by shunning occasions of expense, but by vigorous exertions in time of peace to discharge [pay-off] the debts, which unavoidable wars may have occasioned.

[Do] not selfishly throw the burden upon posterity, which we ourselves ought to bear.

* * * * *

Public Office

Samuel Adams
Letter to his wife October 20, 1778
I know there are many who can serve our Country here with greater Capacity (though none more honestly). The sooner

therefore another is elected in my place the better. I shall the sooner retire to the sweet Enjoyment of domestic Life.

* * * * *

Samuel Adams
Letter to his wife March 7, 1779
Your Wish that I would resign the Office of Secretary perfectly coincides with my own Inclination. I never sought for that or any other Place. Indeed I never was pleased with it, for Reasons which you are not unacquainted with.

* * * * *

George Washington
Letter to John Hancock, January 14, 1776
I have often thought how much happier I should have been, if, instead of accepting of a command under such circumstances, I had taken my musket on my shoulder and entered the ranks, or, if I could have justified the measure to posterity and my own conscience, had retired to the back country, and lived in a wigwam.

* * * * *

George Washington
Letter to Patrick Henry, March 27, 1778
America... has ever had, and I trust she ever will have, my honest exertions to promote her interest. I cannot hope that my services have been the best; but my heart tells me they have been the best that I could render.

* * * * *

Benjamin Franklin
Letter to Robert R. Livingston, December 5, 1784
I am now entering on my 78th year... If I live to see this peace concluded, I shall beg leave to remind the Congress of their promise, then to dismiss me. I shall be happy to sing with old

Simeon, "Now let your servant depart in peace, for mine eyes have seen thy salvation."

* * * * *

Thomas Jefferson
Letter to Alexander Donald February 7, 1788
I had rather be shut up in a very modest cottage with my books, my family and a few old friends, dining on simple bacon, and letting the world roll on as it liked, than to occupy the most splendid post which any human power can give.

* * * * *

George Mason
Letter to a member of the Brent family October 2, 1778
I determined to spend the Remainder of my Days in privacy and Retirement with my Children, from whose Society alone I can expect Comfort.

As mentioned in other places, note the use of the word "society." Society, as it is used here, means "friendly association."

* * * * *

George Mason
Letter to Edmund Randolph October 19, 1782
I quit my Seat in the House of Delegates, from a Conviction that I was no longer able to do any essential Service.

* * * * *

Public Religion

Benjamin Franklin
Proposals Relating to the Education of Youth in Pennsylvania 1749
History will also afford frequent Opportunities of showing the Necessity of a Public Religion, from its Usefulness to the

Public; the Advantage of a Religious Character among private Persons; the Mischiefs of Superstition, etc,. and the Excellency of the Christian Religion above all others, ancient or modern.

* * * * *

The Purpose of America

John Adams
A Dissertation on the Canon and Feudal Law, 1765
I always consider the settlement of America with reverence and wonder, as the opening of a grand scene and design in providence, for the illumination of the ignorant and the emancipation of the slavish part of mankind all over the earth.

* * * * *

Samuel Adams
Speech in Philadelphia August 1, 1776
Our contest is not only whether we ourselves shall be free, but whether there shall be left to mankind an asylum on earth for civil and religious liberty.

* * * * *

Samuel Adams
Letter to Samuel Freeman August 5, 1777
Our Affairs are now in a critical Situation. There is strong Reason however to Promise ourselves by the Assistance of Heaven a favorable Issue.

Men of Virtue throughout Europe heartily wish well to our Cause. They look upon it, as indeed it is, the Cause of Mankind. Liberty seems to be expelled from every other part of the Globe & the Prospect of our affording an Asylum for its Friends in this new World, gives them universal Joy.

Thomas Jefferson

Letter to Roger C. Weightman June 24, 1826

May it be to the world, what I believe it will be (to some parts sooner, to others later, but finally to all), an incitement, arousing men to burst the chains under which monkish ignorance and superstition had persuaded them to bind themselves, and to assume the blessings and security of self-government.

* * * * *

George Washington

Letter to James Warren, March 31, 1779

Our cause is noble; it is the cause of mankind!

* * * * *

George Washington

General Orders April 18, 1783

Happy, thrice happy shall they be pronounced hereafter, who have contributed any thing, who have performed the meanest office in erecting this stupendous fabric of Freedom and Empire on the broad basis of Independency; who have assisted in protecting the rights of humane nature and establishing an Asylum for the poor and oppressed of all nations and religions.

* * * * *

In this fascinating passage, Samuel Adams responds to John Adams, who wonders whether the founding of the United States might be the opening of the millenuium – the thousand year reign with Christ upon earth. (Revelation 20:4)

Samuel Adams

Letter to John Adams October 4, 1790

You ask what the World is about to become? And, Is the Millenium commencing? I have not studied the Prophesies, and cannot even conjecture.

The Golden Age so finely pictured by Poets, I believe has never yet existed; but in their own imaginations. In the earliest periods, when for the honor of human nature, one should have thought that man had not learnt to be cruel; Scenes of horror have been exhibited in families of some of the best instructors in Piety and morals.

Even the heart of our first father [Adam] was grievously wounded at the sight of the murder of one of his Sons [Abel], perpetrated by the hand of the other.

Has Mankind since seen the happy Age? No, my friend. The same Tragedies have been acted on the Theatre of the World, the same Arts of tormenting have been studied, and practiced to this day; and true religion united with reason has never succeeded to establish the permanent foundations of political freedom and happiness in the most enlightened Countries on the Earth.

After a compliment to Boston Town meetings and our Harvard College as having "set the universe in Motion"; you tell me Every Thing will be pulled down. I agree with you that this seems certain, but do you think will be built?

Hay, wood and stubble, will probably be the [building] materials, till Men shall be yet more enlightened, and more friendly to each other.

"Are there any Principles of Political Architecture?" Undoubtedly.

"What are they?" Philosophers ancient, and modern, have laid down different plans, and all have thought themselves to be masters of the true Principles. Their Disciples have followed them, probably with a blind prejudice, which is always an Enemy to truth, and have thereby added fresh fuel to the fire of Contention, and increased the political disorder.

Kings have been deposed by aspiring Nobles, whose pride could not bear restraint.

These have waged everlasting War, against the common rights of Men.

The Love of Liberty is interwoven in the soul of Man, and can never be totally extinguished; and there are certain periods when human patience can no longer endure indignity, and oppression. The spark of liberty then kindles into a flame; when the injured people, attentive to the feelings of their just rights, nobly contend for their complete restoration.

But, such contests have too often ended in nothing more than "a change of deceptions and impositions".

The Patriots of Rome put an End to the Life of Caesar; and Rome submitted to a Race of Tyrants in his stead.

Were the People of England free, after they had obliged King John to concede to them their ancient rights, and Liberties, and promise to govern them according to the Old Law of the Land?

Were they free, after they had recklessly deposed their Henrys, Edwards, and Richards to gratify family pride?

Or, after they had brought their first Charles to the block, and banished his family?

They were not. The Nation was then governed by Kings, Lords, and Commons, and its Liberties were lost by a strife among three Powers, soberly intended to check each other, and keep the scales even.

But while we daily see the violence of the human passions controlling the Laws of Reason and religion, and stifling the very feelings of humanity; can we wonder, that in such tumults little or no regard is paid to Political Checks and Balances?

And such tumults have always happened within as well as without doors. The best formed constitutions that have yet been contrived by the cleverness of Man have, and will come to an End, because "the Kingdoms of the Earth have not been governed by Reason." The Pride of Kings, of Nobles, and leaders of the People who have all governed in their turns have misadjusted the delicate structure, and thrown all into confusion.

What then is to be done? Let Theologians and Philosophers, Statesmen and Patriots unite their endeavors to renovate the Age, by impressing the Minds of Men with the importance of educating their little boys and girls – of instilling in the Minds of youth the fear and Love of the Deity, and universal Philanthropy; and in subordination to these great principles, the Love of their Country; of instructing them in the Art of self government, without which they never can act wisely in the Government of Societies, either great or small.

In short, of leading them in the Study and Practice of the exalted Virtues of the Christian system, which will happily tend to subdue the turbulent passions of Men and introduce that Golden Age beautifully described in figurative language; when the Wolf shall dwell with the Lamb, and the Leopard lie down with the Kid; the Cow and the bear shall feed; their young ones shall lie down together, and the Lion shall eat straw like the Ox—none shall then hurt, or destroy; for the Earth shall be full of the Knowledge of the Lord.

When this Millenium shall commence, if there shall be any need of Civil Government, indulge me in the fancy that it will be in the republican form, or something better.

* * * * *

Rage

John Adams
Personal Diary April 26, 1779
By my physical constitution I am but an ordinary man ... Yet some great events, some cutting expressions, some mean hypocrisies, have at times thrown this assemblage of sloth, sleep, and littleness into rage like a lion.

* * * * *

Reading, Meditation, Discourse

Benjamin Franklin
Poor Richard's Almanac
Reading makes a full Man,
Meditation a profound Man,
discourse a clear Man.

* * * * *

Reason

Thomas Jefferson
Letter to Roger C. Weightman June 24, 1826
The unbounded exercise of reason and freedom of opinion would soon convince all men that they were born not to be ruled - but to rule themselves in freedom.

* * * * *

Thomas Jefferson
Letter to Peter Carr August 10, 1787
You must lay aside all prejudice on both sides, and neither believe nor reject anything, because any other persons, or description of persons, have rejected or believed it.

Your own reason is the only oracle given you by heaven, and you are answerable, not for the rightness, but uprightness of the decision.

In the last line, Jefferson means that we are responsible for deciding uprightly (that is, with integrity), but not for always coming up with the right answer. With our limited knowledge, always finding the right answer is impossible. But the process of deciding with reason and integrity is always available to us.

* * * * *

Thomas Jefferson
Letter to Benjamin Waterhouse July 19, 1822
They might need a preparatory discourse on the text of "prove all things, hold fast that which is good," in order to unlearn the [false] lesson that reason is an unlawful guide in religion.

They might be startled to awake from the dreams of the night, but they would rub their eyes at once, and look the phantoms boldly in the face.

* * * * *

Rebellion

Benjamin Franklin
Proposed Seal of the United States, July, 1776
Moses lifting up his wand, and dividing the Red Sea, and Pharaoh in his chariot overwhelmed with the waters. This motto:

"Rebellion to tyrants is obedience to God."

* * * * *

Thomas Jefferson
Letter to James Madison January 30, 1787
I hold that a little rebellion, now and then, is a good thing, and as necessary in the political world as storms in the physical.

Thomas Jefferson
Letter to William Stephens Smith November 13, 1787
God forbid we should ever be twenty years without such a rebellion.

The people cannot be all, and always, well informed. The part which is wrong will be discontented, in proportion to the importance of the facts they misunderstand. If they remain quiet under such misconceptions, it is lethargy, the forerunner of death to the public liberty.

What country before ever existed a century and half without a rebellion? And what country can preserve its liberties if their rulers are not warned from time to time that their people preserve the spirit of resistance? Let them take arms.

The remedy is to set them right as to facts, pardon and pacify them. What signify a few lives lost in a century or two?

The tree of liberty must be refreshed from time to time with the blood of patriots and tyrants. It is its natural manure.

* * * * *

Here, Samuel Adams points-out something very important: The colonists were not rebelling against the worst government on earth, but against the best. Englishmen had Rights.

Samuel Adams
Boston Gazette, January 21, 1771

For opposing a threatened Tyranny, we have been not only called, but in effect judged Rebels and Traitors to the best of Kings, who has sworn to maintain and defended the Rights and Liberties of his Subjects

We have been represented as harmful to our fellow subjects in Britain, because we have boldly asserted those [same] Rights and Liberties, wherewith they, as Subjects, are made free.

When we complained of this injurious treatment; when we petitioned, and pleaded our grievances, what was the Consequence? Still further indignity; and finally a formal invasion of this town by a fleet and army in the memorable year 1768.

* * * * *

Samuel Adams

Letter to Arthur Lee September 27, 1771

What do you conceive to be the Step next to be taken by an abused people? For another must be taken either by the ministry or the people or in my opinion the nation will fall into that ruin of which they seem to me to be now at the very precipice.

May God afford them that Prudence, Strength and fortitude by which they may be animated to maintain their own Liberties at all Events.

* * * * *

Samuel Adams

Boston Gazette, October 14, 1771

The Tragedy of American Freedom, it is to be feared, is nearly completed: A Tyranny seems to be at the very door.

It is to little purpose then to go about coolly to rehearse the gradual steps that have been taken, the methods that have been used, and the instruments employed, to secure the ruin of the public liberty: We know them and we detest them.

But what will this avail, if we have not courage and resolution to prevent the completion of their system?

* * * * *

Samuel Adams

Boston Gazette, October 14, 1771

The liberties of our Country, the freedom of our civil constitution are worth defending at all hazards: And it is our duty to defend them against all attacks. We have received them as a fair Inheritance from our worthy Ancestors: They purchased them for us with toil and danger and expense of treasure and blood; and transmitted them to us with care and diligence.

It will bring an everlasting mark of infamy on the present generation, enlightened as it is, if we should allow them to be pulled from us by violence, without a struggle; or be cheated out of them by the ingenuity of false and cunning men.

Of the latter we are in most danger at present: Let us therefore be aware of it.

Let us consider our forefathers and our posterity; and resolve to maintain the rights bequeathed to us from the former, for the sake of the latter.

Instead of sitting down satisfied with the efforts we have already made, which is the wish of our enemies, the necessity of the times, more than ever, calls for our utmost forethought, deliberation, strength and perseverance.

Let us remember, that, "if we suffer tamely a lawless attack upon our liberty, we encourage it and involve others in our doom."

It is a very serious consideration, which should deeply impress our minds, that millions yet unborn may be the miserable sharers in the event.

* * * * *

Samuel Adams
Boston Gazette, November 11, 1771

However mystically fawning priests and flatterers may feel about it, Kings and Governors may be guilty of treason and rebellion: And they have, in general in all ages and countries, been more frequently guilty of it than their subjects.

Nay, what has been commonly called rebellion in the people, has often been nothing else but a manly and glorious struggle in opposition to the lawless power of rebellious Kings and Princes; who being elevated above the rest of mankind, and paid by them only to be their protectors, have been taught by enthusiasts to believe they were authorized by God to enslave and butcher them!

* * * * *

Samuel Adams
Letter to Darius Sessions January 2, 1773
I have long feared that this unhappy Contest between Britain and America will end in Rivers of Blood.

Should that be the Case, America I think may wash her hands in Innocence; yet it is the highest prudence to prevent if possible so dreadful a Calamity.

* * * * *

George Washington
Letter to George Mason, April 5, 1769
At a time when our lordly masters in Great Britain will be satisfied with nothing less than the deprivation of American freedom, it seems highly necessary that something should be done to avert the blow, and maintain the liberty which we have derived from our ancestors.

But the manner of doing it, to answer the purpose effectively, is the point in question.

That no man should waver or hesitate a moment to use arms in defense of so valuable a blessing, on which all the good and evil of life depends, is clearly my opinion.

Yet arms, if you will permit me to add, should be the last resource, the final resort.

Addresses to the throne, and pleas to Parliament, we have already proved to be useless.

How far, then, their attention to our rights and privileges is to be awakened or alarmed by starving their trade and manufacturing remains to be tried.

* * * * *

Thomas Jefferson
Declaration of Independence 1776
Whenever any Form of Government becomes destructive of these ends [life, liberty, the pursuit of happiness], it is the Right of the people to alter or abolish it.

Rebellion, Not To Be Delayed

James Madison
Memorial and Remonstrance Against Religious Assessments 1785
The free men of America did not wait till usurped power had strengthened itself by exercise, and entangled the question in precedents.

They saw all the consequences in the principle, and they avoided the consequences of denying the principle.

We revere this lesson too much to quickly forget it.

* * * * *

Patrick Henry
Second Virginia Convention March 23, 1775
They tell us, sir, that we are weak; unable to cope with so formidable an adversary. But when shall we be stronger? Will it be the next week, or the next year? Will it be when we are totally disarmed, and when a British guard shall be stationed in every house?

Shall we gather strength by indecision and inaction?

Shall we acquire the tools of effective resistance by lying passively on our backs and hugging the delusive phantom of hope, until our enemies shall have bound us hand and foot?

* * * * *

Reformers

Jefferson expresses the truth that those who labor to improve mankind are punished for their efforts.

Thomas Jefferson
Letter to James Ogilvie August 4, 1811
Politics, like religion, hold up the torches of martyrdom to the reformers of error.

* * * * *

Religion

Benjamin Franklin
Poor Richard's Almanac 1743
How many observe Christ's birth-day! How few, his precepts! O! 'tis easier to keep Holidays than Commandments.

* * * * *

Samuel Adams
The Rights Of The Colonists 1772
In regard to Religion, mutual toleration in the different professions thereof is what all good and candid minds in all ages have practiced; and both by precept and example inculcated on mankind:

It is now generally agreed among Christians that this spirit of toleration in the fullest extent consistent with the existence of civil society is the chief characteristic of the true church.

* * * * *

Samuel Adams
The Rights Of The Colonists November 20, 1772
As neither reason requires, nor religion permits the contrary, every Man, living in or out of a state of civil society, has a right peaceably and quietly to worship God according to the dictates of his conscience.

* * * * *

Samuel Adams
Letter to Stephan Collins January 31, 1775
It is also a Misrepresentation that the sect taken notice of for opening their Shops on our late Thanksgiving Day, was that of the People called Quakers.

These were the Disciples of the late Mr. Sanderman, who worship God here without the least molestation according to their own manner, and are in no other light disregarded here but as it is said they are in general avowed Friends of the Ministerial Measures.

This is what I am told, for my own part I know but little or nothing about them. The Different denominations of Christians here (excepting those amongst them who espouse the cause of our enemies) are in perfect peace and Harmony, as I trust they always will be.

* * * * *

James Madison
Letter to William Bradford, April 1, 1774
Religious bondage shackles and debilitates the mind and disqualifies it for every noble enterprise, every expanded prospect.

* * * * *

Thomas Jefferson
Bill to Establish Religious Freedom 1779
The prohibiting any citizen as unworthy of the public confidence, by forbidding him to be called to offices of trust or compensation, unless he profess or renounce this or that religions opinion, is to unwisely deprive him of those privileges and advantages to which, in common with his fellow-citizens, he has a natural right.

It tends also to corrupt the principles of that very religion it is meant to encourage, by bribing it with a monopoly on worldly honors and payments.

* * * * *

Thomas Jefferson
Letter to Peter Carr August 10, 1787
Your reason is now mature enough to examine this object [religion].

In the first place divest yourself of all bias in favor of novelty & singularity of opinion. Indulge them in any other subject rather than that of religion. It is too important, & the consequences of error may be too serious.

On the other hand shake off all the fears & servile prejudices under which weak minds are submissively crouched. Fix reason firmly in her seat, and call to her tribunal every fact, every opinion.

Question with boldness even the existence of a god; because, if there be one, he must more approve the homage of reason, than that of blindfolded fear.

* * * * *

Thomas Jefferson
Letter to the Danbury Baptist Association January 1, 1802
I believe with you that religion is a matter which lies solely between man and his God, that he owes an account to no other for his faith or his worship.

[I believe] that the legislative powers of government extend to actions only, and not opinions.

I contemplate with sovereign reverence that act of the whole American people which declared that their legislature should "make no law respecting an establishment of religion, or prohibiting the free exercise thereof," thus building a wall of separation between church and State.

* * * * *

Thomas Jefferson
Letter to Richard Rush 1813
Religion is a subject on which I have ever been most scrupulously reserved. I have considered it as a matter between every man and his Maker in which no other, and far less the public, had a right to intermeddle.

* * * * *

Thomas Jefferson
Letter to John Adams January 11, 1817
Say nothing of my religion. It is known to my God and myself alone.

* * * * *

Thomas Jefferson
Letter to Albert Gallatin 16 June 1817
The Pennsylvania legislature, who, on a proposal to make the belief in God a necessary qualification for office, rejected it by a great majority, although assuredly there was not a single atheist in their assembly.

And you remember to have heard, that when the act for religious freedom was before the Virginia Assembly, a motion to insert the name of Jesus Christ before the phrase, "the author of our holy religion," which stood in the bill, was rejected, although that was the creed of a great majority of them.

John Adams

Letter to Thomas Jefferson April 19, 1817

Twenty times in the course of my recent reading have I been on the point of breaking out, "This would be the best of all possible worlds, if there were no religion in it!!!"

But in this exclamation I would have been as fanatical as Bryant or Cleverly. Without religion this world would be something not fit to be mentioned in polite company, I mean Hell.

* * * * *

George Washington

General Orders May 2, 1778

While we are zealously performing the duties of good citizens and soldiers, we certainly ought not to be inattentive to the higher duties of religion.

To the distinguished character of Patriot, it should be our highest glory to add the more distinguished character of Christian.

* * * * *

James Madison

Letter to Rev. Frederick Beasley November 20, 1825

The belief in a God All Powerful wise and good, is so essential to the moral order of the world and to the happiness of man, that arguments which enforce it cannot be drawn from too many sources nor adapted with too much concern for the different characters and capacities to be impressed with it.

* * * * *

Religion, Necessity Of

Benjamin Franklin

Letter to unknown recipient 13 December 1757

I have read your Manuscript with some Attention. By the Arguments it contains against the Doctrine of a particular Providence, though you allow a general Providence, you strike at the Foundation of all Religion: For without the Belief of a Providence that takes Cognizance of, guards and guides and may favor particular Persons, there is no Motive to Worship a Deity, to fear its Displeasure, or to pray for its Protection.

I will not enter into any Discussion of your Principles, though' you seem to desire it; At present I shall only give you my Opinion that though your Reasoning are subtle, and may prevail with some Readers, you will not succeed so as to change the general Sentiments of Mankind on that Subject, and the Consequence of printing this Piece will be a great deal of Odium drawn upon your self, Mischief to you and no Benefit to others.

He that spits against the wind, spits in his own face. But were you to succeed, do you imagine any Good would be done by it?

You yourself may find it easy to live a virtuous Life without the Assistance afforded by Religion; you having a clear Perception of the Advantages of Virtue and the Disadvantages of Vice, and possessing a Strength of Resolution sufficient to enable you to resist common Temptations. But think how great a Proportion of Mankind consists of weak and ignorant Men and Women, and of inexperienced and inconsiderate Youth of both Sexes, who have need of the Motives of Religion to restrain them from Vice, to support their Virtue, and retain them in the Practice of it till it becomes habitual, which is the great Point for its Security.

And perhaps you are indebted to her originally. That is, [indebted] to your Religious Education, for the Habits of Virtue upon which you now justly value yourself.

You might easily display your excellent Talents of reasoning on a less hazardous Subject, and thereby obtain Rank with our most distinguished Authors.

For among us, it is not necessary, as among the Hottentots that a Youth to be received into the Company of Men, should prove his Manhood by beating his Mother.

I would advise you therefore not to attempt unchaining the Tiger, but to burn this Piece before it is seen by any other Person, whereby you will save yourself a great deal of Mortification from the Enemies it may raise against you, and perhaps a good deal of Regret and Repentance.

If Men are so wicked as we now see them with Religion what would they be if without it?

* * * * *

Religion And State

Madison maintains that to mix religion and government is to degrade them both. Government and morality (the subject of religion) operate on differing principles: Morality involves choices, but government involves coercion. These negate each other. (See Madison's quote under "Coercion.")

James Madison
Letter to Edward Livingston July 10, 1822
Religion and Government will both exist in greater purity, the less they are mixed together.

* * * * *

James Madison
Memorial and Remonstrance Against Religious Assessments 1785
During almost fifteen centuries has the legal establishment of Christianity been on trial. What have been its fruits? More or less in all places, pride and indolence in the Clergy, ignorance and servility in the laity, in both, superstition, bigotry and persecution.

* * * * *

Religious Freedom

James Madison
Memorial and Remonstrance Against Religious Assessments 1785
The Religion then of every man must be left to the conviction and conscience of every man; and it is the right of every man to exercise it as these may dictate. This right is in its nature an unalienable right.

It is unalienable because the opinions of men, depending only on the evidence contemplated by their own minds, cannot follow the dictates of other men.

It is unalienable also because this right is a duty towards the Creator.

We maintain therefore that in matters of Religion, no man's right is abridged by the institution of Civil Society, and that Religion is wholly exempt from its cognizance.

* * * * *

George Mason
Virginia Declaration of Rights 1776
Religion, or the duty which we owe to our Creator and the manner of discharging it, can be directed by reason and conviction, not by force or violence; and therefore, all men are equally entitled to the free exercise of religion, according to the dictates of conscience; and that it is the mutual duty of

all to practice Christian forbearance, love, and charity towards each other.

* * * * *

Repentance

Benjamin Franklin
Poor Richard's Almanac
Many Princes sin with David, but few repent with him.

Franklin's reference is to the story of David and Bathsheba, from the second Book of Samuel.

* * * * *

Benjamin Franklin
Poor Richard's Almanac
He that resolves to mend hereafter, resolves not to mend now.

* * * * *

Reproof

The founders seldom used rebuke or reproof, both for their own sakes and for reasons of practicality. On occasion, however, they used it with force.

The following quote from Washington is to a group of soldiers who were beginning a rebellion at the end of the war. They had very legitimate complaints, but were going about to correct them in a very wrong and dangerous way.

George Washington
Letter to Officers of the Army, March 12, 1783
Can you then consent to be the only sufferers by this revolution, and retiring from the field, grow old in poverty, wretchedness and contempt? Can you consent to wade

through the vile mire of dependency, and owe the miserable remnant of that life to charity, which has hitherto been spent in honor? If you can - GO - and carry with you the jest of tories and scorn of whigs - the ridicule, and what is worse, the pity of the world. Go, starve, and be forgotten!

* * * * *

Here, Samuel Adams speaks to a crowd shortly after the Declaration of Independence was published.

Samuel Adams
Speech in Philadelphia August 1, 1776
If you love wealth better than liberty, the tranquility of servitude than the animated contest of freedom — go home from us in peace. We ask not your counsels or arms. Crouch down and lick the hands which feed you. May your chains sit lightly upon you, and may posterity forget that you were our countrymen!

* * * * *

The Republic, An Experiment

A Republic was a strange idea at the founding of America. All of western Europe was ruled by kings, and had been for a millennium. To institute a Republic was a radical plan. And since the Roman Republic had so famously failed, it was a plan that was easy to criticize. It was a quite uncertain experiment.

George Washington
First Inaugural Address April 30, 1789
The preservation of the sacred fire of liberty, and the destiny of the republican model of government, are justly considered as deeply, and perhaps finally, staked on the experiment entrusted to the American people.

* * * * *

Reputation

George Washington
Formal acceptance of command of the Army June 16, 1775
But lest some unlucky event should happen unfavorable to my reputation, I beg it may be remembered by every gentleman in the room that I this day declare with the utmost sincerity, I do not think myself equal to the command I am honored with.

* * * * *

George Washington
Letter to Col. Burwell Bassett, his brother-in-law, June 19, 1775
Reputation derives its principal support from success.

* * * * *

Restoration

The second term of George Washington and the Presidency of John Adams were seen by very many Americans as openly contrary to the principles they had fought Britain to preserve. These people, Sam Adams among them, were greatly relieved that Jefferson would be President, and would turn things back around. (And to a very considerable extent, he did.)

Samuel Adams
Letter to Thomas Jefferson April 24, 1801
No man can be fit to sustain an office who cannot consent to the principles by which he must be governed. With you, I hope, we shall once more see harmony restored.

But after so severe and long a storm, it will take a proportionate time to still the raging of the waves. The World has been governed by prejudice and passion, which never can be friendly to truth; and while you nobly resolve to retain the principles of candor and of justice, resulting from a free elective Representative Government (which they have been taught to hate and despise), you must depend upon being hated yourself, because they hate your principles.

Not a man of them will dare openly to despise you: Your inaugural speech, to say nothing of your eminent services to the acceptance of our Country, will secure you from contempt.

[But] it may require some time before the great body of our fellow citizens will settle in harmony good humor and peace. When deep prejudices shall be removed in some, the self interestedness of others shall cease and many honest men, whose minds have been clouded by a lack of good information, shall return to the use of their own understanding. [Then] the happy and wished-for time will come.

The Eyes of the people have too generally been tightly closed from the view of their own happiness, this, alas, has always been the lot of Man!

But Providence, who rules the World, seems now to be rapidly changing the sentiments of Mankind in Europe and America.

* * * * *

The Revolution

John Adams
Letter to Thomas Jefferson August 24, 1815
What do we mean by the Revolution? The war? That was no part of the revolution; it was only an effect and consequence of it.

The revolution was in the minds of the people, and this was effected from 1760-1775, in the course of fifteen years, before a drop of blood was shed at Lexington.

See Adams' quote under Christianity for an example of the changing opinions of that time. In another place, Adams names a particular sermon that circulated widely in the 1750s ("A Discourse Concerning Unlimited Submission and Non-Resistance to the Higher Powers," by Jonathan Mayhew) and claims that this was "the spark that ignited the American Revolution."

* * * * *

John Adams
Letter to Hezekiah Niles February 13, 1818

By what means this great and important alteration in the religious, moral, political, and social character of the people of thirteen colonies, all distinct, unconnected, and independent of each other, was begun, pursued, and accomplished, it is surely interesting to humanity to investigate, and perpetuate to posterity.

To this end, it is greatly to be desired, that young men of letters in all the States, especially in the thirteen original States, would undertake the laborious, but certainly interesting and amusing task, of searching and collecting all the records, pamphlets, newspapers, and even handbills, which in any way contributed to change the temper and views of the people, and compose them into an independent nation.

* * * * *

George Washington
Circular to the States, 1783

It is yet to be decided whether the Revolution must ultimately be considered as a blessing or a curse.

A blessing or a curse, not to the present age alone, for with our fate will the destiny of unborn millions be involved.

* * * * *

To this day, some people claim that the American Revolution was the work of a few rich, educated men, who pursued it for their own selfish reasons. George Mason takes-on this claim directly:

George Mason
Letter to a member of the Brent family October 2, 1778
There never was an idler or a falser Notion than that which the British Ministry have imposed upon the Nation "that this great Revolution has been the Work of a Faction, of a Junta of ambitious Men against the Sense of the People of America."

On the Contrary, nothing has been done without the Approbation of the People, who have indeed out-run their Leaders; so that no serious measure hath been adopted, until they called loudly for it.

To any one who knows Mankind, there needs no greater Proof than the cordial Manner in which they have co-operated, and the Patience and Perseverance with which they have struggled under their Sufferings; which have been greater than you, at a Distance, can conceive, or I describe.

Equally false is the Assertion that Independence was originally planned. Things have gone to such lengths, that it is a matter of nonsense to us, whether Independence was at first intended or not...

The truth is, we have been forced into it, as the only means of self-preservation, to guard our country and posterity from the greatest of all Evils: An infernal Government (if it deserves the Name of Government) as the Provinces groaned under in the latter Ages of the Roman Commonwealth.

* * * * *

Thomas Jefferson
Letter to John Adams September 12, 1821
Should the cloud of barbarism and despotism again obscure the science and libraries of Europe, this country remains to preserve and restore light and liberty to them.

In short, the flames kindled on the fourth of July, 1776, have spread over too much of the globe to be extinguished by the feeble engines of despotism; on the contrary, they will consume these engines and all who work them.

*****

Jefferson, nearly fifty years after independence was declared, has decided that they did not fully live up to the moment that was presented to them. Specifically, he thinks that alternate methods should have been used to break up cabals (plotters, parties, factions) in the legislatures.

Thomas Jefferson
Letter to John Cartwright, 1824
Our Revolution presented us an album on which we were free to write what we pleased. Yet we did not avail ourselves of all the advantages of our position.

[Previously,] we had never been permitted to exercise self-government. When forced to assume it, we were novices in its science. Its principles and forms had little entered into our former education. We established, however, some (but not all) of its important principles.

The constitutions of most of our States assert that all power is inherent in the people; that they may exercise it by themselves, in all cases to which they think themselves competent (as in electing their executive and legislative functionaries, deciding by a jury of themselves, in all judicial cases in which any fact is involved), or they may act by representatives, freely and equally chosen; that it is their right and duty to be at all times armed; that they are entitled to freedom of person, freedom of religion, freedom of property, and freedom of the press.

In the structure of our legislatures, we think experience has proved the benefit of subjecting questions to two separate bodies of deliberants.

But in constituting these bodies, [we have] been mistaken, making one of these bodies, and in some cases both, the representatives of property instead of persons.

This double deliberation might be obtained just as well without any violation of true principle, either by requiring a greater age in one of the bodies, or by electing a proper number of representatives of persons, or by dividing them by lots into two chambers, and renewing the division at frequent intervals, in order to break up all cabals.

* * * * *

Rights

As mentioned under "Americans" and "Courage & Cowardice," the colonists' theories of natural rights came from John Locke. This was fundamental to them. Without Locke's great works on this subject, there would have been no American Revolution in the late 18th Century… at least not in a form we would recognize.

Samuel Adams
The Rights of the Colonists, November 20, 1772
Among the natural rights of the Colonists are these: First, a right to life; Secondly, to liberty; Thirdly, to property; together with the right to support and defend them in the best manner they can.

These are evident branches of, rather than deductions from, the duty of self-preservation, commonly called the first law of nature.

* * * * *

Samuel Adams
Letter to John Wadsworth April 13 1773
We wish for & hope soon to see that Union of Sentiments in the several Towns throughout this province and in the

American Colonies which shall strike a Terror in the hearts of those who would enslave us.

And together with a Spirit of union may God inspire us with that ardent Zeal for the support of religious and civil Liberty which animated the Breasts of the first Settlers of the old Colony of Plymouth from whom the native Inhabitants of Duxborough have lineally descended.

After the Example of those renowned Heroes, whose memory we revere, let us gloriously defend our Rights and Liberties, and resolve to transmit the fair Inheritance they purchased for us with Treasure and Blood to their last posterity.

* * * * *

Samuel Adams
The Rights Of The Colonists November 20, 1772
All Men have a Right to remain in a State of Nature as long as they please; and in case of intolerable Oppression, Civil or Religious, to leave the Society they belong to, and enter into another.

When Men enter into Society, it is by voluntary consent.

* * * * *

Samuel Adams
Boston Gazette, July 22, 1771
Here is the most unreasonable and unjust distinction, made between the subjects in Britain and America; as though it were designed to exclude us from the least share in that clause of Magna-Charta, which has for many centuries been the noblest bulwark of the English liberties, and which cannot be too often repeated: "No freeman shall be taken or imprisoned or disseized of his freehold [have his property confiscated], or liberties, or free customs, or be outlawed, or exiled, or any otherwise destroyed, nor will we pass upon him nor condemn him, but by the judgment of his peers or the law of the land."

Samuel Adams
Letter to Stephen Sayre, November 16, 1770

The People here are holding tightly to their just Rights and I hope in God they will always firmly maintain them. Every Attempt to enforce the plan of Despotism will certainly irritate them.

While they have a Sense of freedom they will oppose the Efforts of Tyranny; and although the Mother Country may at present boast of her Superiority over them, she may perhaps find a lack of Superiority, when by repeated provocations she shall have totally lost their Affections.

* * * * *

Samuel Adams
Letter to Arthur Lee September 27, 1771

With Regard the Grievances of the Americans it must be acknowledged that the Violation of the essential Right of taxing themselves is an extremely serious one.

This Right is founded in Nature. It is unalienable & therefore it belongs to us exclusively. The least Infringement on it is Sacrilege.

* * * * *

Samuel Adams
Boston Gazette, December 23, 1771

Remember my countrymen, it will be better to have your liberties ripped from you by force, than to have it said that you even implicitly surrendered them.

By "implicitly," Adams means surrendering rights without ever admitting it.

* * * * *

Samuel Adams
The Rights Of The Colonists November 20, 1772

In the state of nature, every man is under God, Judge and sole Judge, of his own rights and the injuries done him.

By entering into society, he agrees to an Arbiter or indifferent Judge between him and his neighbors; but he no more renounces his original right, than he would by withholding a case from of the ordinary courts, and giving it to other Referees or Arbitrators.

In the last case he must pay the Referees for time and trouble; he should be also willing to pay his just quota for the support of government, the law and constitution; the purpose of which is to furnish indifferent and impartial Judges in all cases that may arise, whether civil, ecclesiastical, marine or military.

As mentioned in other places, Adams does not write "A society," as if it were an external set of rules men must conform to – but simply "society," meaning "a friendly association with others."

* * * * *

Mason maintains that even if a generation agrees to cede some of its rights, this is not binding upon their children. Every generation and every individual must separately agree to their arrangements. All else is tyranny against their inherent rights.

George Mason
Virginia Declaration of Rights 1776
All men are by nature equally free and independent, and have certain inherent rights, of which, when they enter into a state of society, they cannot, by any agreement, deprive or divest their posterity; namely, the enjoyment of life and liberty, with the means of acquiring and possessing property, and pursuing and obtaining happiness and safety.

* * * * *

Samuel Adams
The Rights Of The Colonists November 20, 1772
In short it is the greatest absurdity to suppose that it is in the power of one or any number of men, at their entering into

society, to renounce their essential natural rights, or their methods of preserving those rights when the great end of civil government, from the very nature of its institution, is for the support, protection and defense of those very rights: the principal of which, as previously observed, are life liberty and property.

If men, through fear, fraud or mistake, should renounce and give up any essential natural right, the eternal law of reason and the great end of society, would absolutely vacate such a renunciation.

The right to freedom being the gift of God Almighty, it is not in the power of Man to alienate this gift, and to voluntarily become a slave.

* * * * *

Samuel Adams
The Rights Of The Colonists November 20, 1772
The absolute Rights of Englishmen, and all freemen in or out of Civil society, are principally, personal security personal liberty and private property.

* * * * *

Samuel Adams
Independent Chronicle, January 20, 1794
Is easy to conceive that men, naturally formed for society, were inclined to enter into mutual compact for the better security of their natural rights.

In this state of society, the unalienable rights of nature are held sacred, and each member is entitled to an equal share of all the social rights.

No man can rightly become possessed of a greater share: If any one usurps it, he so far becomes a tyrant; and when he can obtain sufficient strength, the people will feel the rod of a tyrant.

Or, if this exclusive privilege [usurping the rights of others] is supposed to be secured by the power of an agreement, it is a very serious defect. The people, when more enlightened, will alter their agreement, and extinguish the very idea.

* * * * *

John Adams
Dissertation on Canon & Feudal Law 1765
I say Rights, for they have them, undoubtedly, prior to all earthly government – Rights that cannot be repealed or restrained by human laws – Rights derived from the great Legislator of the universe.

* * * * *

Thomas Jefferson
Declaration of Independence 1776
We hold these truths to be self-evident, that all men are created equal; that they are endowed by their Creator with inherent and inalienable Rights; that among these, are Life, Liberty, and the pursuit of Happiness; that to secure these rights, Governments are instituted among Men, deriving their just powers from the consent of the governed.

* * * * *

Thomas Jefferson
Letter to Francis W. Gilmer June 27, 1816
Our legislators are not sufficiently apprized of the rightful limits of their power; that their true office is to declare and enforce only our natural rights and duties, and to take none of them from us.

No man has a natural right to commit aggression on the equal rights of another; and this is all from which the laws ought to restrain him.

Every man is under the natural duty of contributing to the necessities of the society; and this is all the laws should enforce on him.

And, no man having a natural right to be the judge between himself and another, it is his natural duty to submit to the arbitration of an impartial third party.

When the laws have declared and enforced all this, they have fulfilled their functions, and the idea is quite unfounded, that on entering into society we give up any natural right.

* * * * *

Thomas Jefferson
Letter to Roger C. Weightman (his last) June 24, 1826
All eyes are opened, or opening, to the rights of man. The general spread of the light of science has already laid open to every view the palpable truth, that the mass of mankind has not been born with saddles on their backs, nor a favored few [born] booted and spurred, ready to ride them legitimately, by the grace of God.

* * * * *

Here, early in the war, Hamilton writes in favor of natural rights.

Alexander Hamilton
The Farmer Refuted 1775
The sacred rights of mankind are not to be rummaged for among old parchments or musty records. They are written, as with a sunbeam, in the whole volume of human nature, by the hand of the divinity itself; and can never be erased or obscured by mortal power.

* * * * *

Years later, while promoting the new Constitution, Hamilton that claims that rights cannot be separated from government. And he goes further, saying that zeal for the rights of the people is more dangerous than a zeal for a strong government.

Alexander Hamilton
Federalist #1
it will be equally forgotten that the vigor of government is essential to the security of liberty; that, in the contemplation of a sound and well-informed judgment, their interest can never be separated; and that a dangerous ambition more often lurks behind the false mask of zeal for the rights of the people than under the forbidden appearance of zeal for the firmness and efficiency of government.

* * * * *

Rules

Thomas Jefferson
Letter to Peter Carr August 10, 1787
State a moral case to a ploughman and a professor. The former will decide it as well, and often better than the latter, because he has not been led astray by artificial rules.

* * * * *

Secrets

Benjamin Franklin
Poor Richard's Almanac
To whom thy secret thou dost tell,
to him thy freedom thou dost sell.

* * * * *

Benjamin Franklin
Poor Richard's Almanac
Three may keep a secret, if two of them be dead.

* * * * *

Secret Societies

Here Sam Adams praises the Sons of Liberty for their bravery in opposing the Stamp Act. The Sons of Liberty were underground groups that functioned in nearly every colony, composed mainly of the more productive men: merchants, artisans, traders, etc. The British authorities derided them as the "Sons of Violence" or the "Sons of Iniquity."

Samuel Adams
Boston Gazette, August 19, 1771
We cannot surely have forgot the accursed designs of a most detestable set of men, to destroy the Liberties of America as with one blow, by the Stamp-Act; nor the noble and successful efforts we then made to divert the impending stroke of ruin aimed at ourselves and our posterity.

The Sons of Liberty on the 14th of August 1765, a Day which ought to be for ever remembered in America, animated with a zeal for their country then upon the brink of destruction. Resolved to save her, or like Samson to perish in the ruins, they exerted themselves with such distinguished vigor, as to shake the house of Dogon from its very foundation; and the hopes of the lords of the Philistines even while their hearts were merry, and when they were anticipating the joy of plundering this continent, were at that very time buried in the pit they dug.

The People shouted, and their shout was heard to the distant end of this Continent. In each Colony they deliberated and resolved, and every Stampman trembled; and swore by his Maker, that he would never execute a commission which he had so infamously received.

* * * * *

Franklin describes his intellectually-oriented private society, the Junto. (Which, in modern terms, means "the cabal.")

Benjamin Franklin
His Autobiography, 1774

Our club, the Junto, was found so useful, and afforded such satisfaction to the members, that several were desirous of introducing their friends, which could not well be done without exceeding what we had settled as a convenient number, that is, twelve. We had from the beginning made it a rule to keep our institution a secret, which was well observed. The intention was to avoid applications of improper persons for admittance, some of whom, perhaps, we might find it difficult to refuse.

I was one of those who were against any addition to our number, but, instead of it, made in writing a proposal, that every member separately should endeavor to form a subordinate club, with the same rules respecting queries, etc., and without informing them of the connection with the Junto.

The advantages proposed were the improvement of so many more young citizens by the use of our institutions; our better acquaintance with the general sentiments of the inhabitants on any occasion, as the Junto member might propose what questions we should desired, and was to report to the Junto what transpired in his separate club; the promotion of our particular interests in business by more extensive recommendation, and the increase of our influence in public affairs, and our power of doing good by spreading the sentiments of the Junto through the various clubs.

The project was approved, and every member undertook to form his club, but they did not all succeed. Five or six only were completed, which were called by different names, such as the Vine, the Union, the Band, etc. They were useful to themselves, and afforded us a good deal of amusement, information, and instruction, besides answering, in some considerable degree, our views of influencing the public opinion on particular occasions, of which I shall give some instances in course of time as they happened.

* * * * *

Some rules of the Junto.

Benjamin Franklin
His Autobiography, 1771

I had gathered most of my ingenious acquaintance into a club of mutual improvement, which we called the Junto; we met on Friday evenings.

The rules that I drew up required that every member, in his turn, should produce one or more queries on any point of Morals, Politics, or Natural Philosophy, to be discussed by the company; and once in three months produce and read an essay of his own writing, on any subject he pleased.

Our debates were to be under the direction of a president, and to be conducted in the sincere spirit of inquiry after truth, without fondness for dispute, or desire of victory. And, to prevent warmth, all expressions of approval in opinions, or direct contradiction, were after some time made contraband, and prohibited under small pecuniary penalties.

* * * * *

Plans for a secret society that was never completed, called The Society of the Free and Easy.

Benjamin Franklin
His Autobiography, 1774

My ideas at that time were, that the sect should be begun and spread at first among young and single men only; that each person to be initiated should not only declare his assent to such creed, but should have exercised himself with the thirteen weeks' examination and practice of the virtues, as in the before-mentioned model.

[Also] that the existence of such a society should be kept a secret, till it was become considerable, to prevent requests for the admission from improper persons, but that each of the members should search among his acquaintance for ingenuous, well-disposed youths, to whom, with prudent caution, the scheme should be gradually communicated; that the members should engage to afford their advice, assistance, and support to each other in promoting one another's interests, business, and advancement in life.

[We decided] that, for distinction, we should be called The Society of the Free and Easy: Free, as being, by the general practice and habit of the virtues, free from the dominion of vice; and particularly by the practice of industry and frugality, free from debt, which exposes a man to confinement, and a species of slavery to his creditors.

This is as much as I can now recollect of the project, except that I communicated it in part to two young men, who adopted it with some enthusiasm; but my then narrow circumstances, and the necessity I was under of sticking close to my business, occasioned my postponing the further development of it at that time; and my many occupations, public and private, induced me to continue postponing, so that it has been omitted till I have no longer strength or activity left sufficient for such an enterprise; though I am still of opinion that it was a practicable scheme, and might have been very useful, by forming a great number of good citizens.

I was not discouraged by the seeming magnitude of the undertaking, as I have always thought that one man of tolerable abilities may work great changes, and accomplish great affairs among mankind, if he first forms a good plan, and, cutting off all amusements or other employments that would divert his attention, makes the execution of that same plan his sole study and business.

* * * * *

Self-Government

John Adams
Letter to his wife May 17, 1776

There is something very unnatural and odious in a government a thousand leagues off.

A whole government of our own choice, managed by persons whom we love, revere, and can confide in, has charms in it for which men will fight.

* * * * *

Self-Interest

Samuel Adams
Letter to his wife January 29, 1777

There is indeed no such thing as disinterested benevolence among men. Self love and social, as Pope tells us, is the same.

The truly charitable man partakes of the feelings of the wretched wherever he sees the object, and he relieves himself from misery by relieving others.

"Pope" is Alexander Pope, the English poet.

* * * * *

Self-Responsibility

Thomas Jefferson
Notes on Religion 1776

The care of every man's soul belongs to himself. But what if he neglect the care of it?

Well, what if he neglect the care of his health or his estate? ...

Will the magistrate make a law that he is not poor or sick?

Laws provide against injury from others; but not from ourselves. God himself will not save men against their wills.

The Senate

Here, John Adams expresses a thought that is strange to modern observers, but was not uncommon at the time: That the Senate should be the house of the rich and well-born.

John Adams
Defense of the Constitutions of Government 1787
The rich, the well-born, and the able acquire an influence among the people that will soon be too much for simple honesty and plain sense, in a house of representatives. The most illustrious of them must, therefore, be separated from the mass, and placed by themselves in a senate; this is, to all honest and useful intents, an ostracism.

* * * * *

Here, Madison specifies that the Senate derives its powers from the states, not from the people.

James Madison
Federalist #39
The Senate, on the other hand, will derive its powers from the States, as political and coequal societies; and these will be represented on the principle of equality in the Senate, as they now are in the existing Congress. So far the government is Federal, not National.

* * * * *

Separation

Sam Adams explains that America had previously been an obscure place to which people escaped, and that they were happy in that state. In other words, they had no desire to challenge or defeat the British; they only wanted to be left alone to pursue their own ways of life.

Samuel Adams
Letter to John Wilkes, December 28, 1770
In this little part of the world - a land, until recently happy in its obscurity - the asylum, to which Patriots were accustomed to make their peaceful Retreat; even here, the stern Tyrant has lifted up his iron Rod, and makes his incessant Claim as Lord of the Soil.

But I have a firm Persuasion in my Mind, that in every Struggle, this Country will approve her self as glorious in defending and maintaining her Freedom, as she has heretofore been happy in enjoying it.

* * * * *

Sin

Benjamin Franklin
Poor Richard's Almanac
Sin is not hurtful because it is forbidden but it is forbidden because it's hurtful.

* * * * *

Slavery, Slaves

Slavery was rightly said to have been "the great unfinished work of the revolution." Getting rid of such a huge, entrenched system, however, was much more difficult than it might seem. While it was certainly a gigantic evil, undoing things of such size and age is difficult.

In this first quote, Washington notes some of his difficulties.

George Washington
Letter to Robert Lewis, August 18, 1799
It is demonstratively clear that on this Estate I have more working Negroes by a full half than can be employed to any advantage in the farming system… Half the workers I keep on this estate would provide me greater profit than I now derive from the whole…

I cannot sell the extra, because I am principled against this kind of traffic in the human species. To hire them out is almost as bad because they could not be disposed of in families to any advantage, and to break up the families I have an aversion.

* * * * *

The Marquis de Lafayette and Washington work on schemes for emancipating the slaves:

George Washington
Letter to the Marquis de Lafayette, April 5, 1785
The scheme, my dear Marquis, which you propose as a precedent, to encourage the emancipation of the black people of this Country from that state of Bondage in which they are held, is a striking evidence of the benevolence of your Heart. I shall be happy to join you in so laudable a work.

* * * * *

Thomas Jefferson
Draft of the Declaration of Independence, 1776
He [the king of England] has waged cruel war against human nature itself, violating its most sacred rights of life and liberty in the persons of a distant people who never offended him, captivating and carrying them into slavery in another hemisphere, or to incur miserable death in their transportation thither.

This piratical warfare, the disgrace of an infidel's powers, is the warfare of the Christian king of Great Britain.... suppressing every legislative attempt to prohibit or to restrain this execrable commerce, determining to keep open a market where Men should be bought and sold.

* * * * *

James Madison
Letter to Richard Henry Lee, July 17, 1785
Another of my wishes is to depend as little as possible on the labor of slaves.

* * * * *

Madison explains why the framers of the constitution did not use the word "slave," and used "other persons" instead.

James Madison
Farrand's Records of the Federal Convention of 1787, August 25, 1787
The Convention thought it wrong to admit in the Constitution the idea that there could be property in men.

* * * * *

George Mason
Virginia Charters, July, 1773
Taught to regard a part of our own Species in the most abject and contemptible Degree below us, we lose that Idea of the

dignity of Man which the Hand of Nature had implanted in us, for great and useful purposes.

* * * * *

George Mason
Virginia Ratifying Convention June 17, 1788
The augmentation of slaves weakens the states; and such a trade is diabolical in itself, and disgraceful to mankind.

* * * * *

George Mason
Virginia Ratifying Convention June 17, 1788
As much as I value a union of all the states, I would not admit the southern states into the union, unless they agreed to the discontinuance of this disgraceful trade, because it would bring weakness and not strength to the union.

* * * * *

Thomas Jefferson
Letter to Edward Coles August 25, 1814
The hour of emancipation is advancing... this enterprise is for the young; for those who can follow it up, and bear it through to its conclusion.

It shall have all my prayers, and these are the only weapons of an old man.

* * * * *

Thomas Jefferson
Autobiography 1821
Nothing is more certainly written in the book of fate, than that these people are to be free; nor is it less certain that the two races, equally free, cannot live in the same government. Nature, habit, opinion have drawn indelible lines of distinction between them.

Solidarity

Adams tells the story of the merchants of New York shutting their port, rather than allowing the British to ruin the port of Boston. These merchants stood to make money on the deal (Boston and New York were competitive ports), but to do so would be to profit by the immoral use of force. They turned down the profits and stood with Boston.

Samuel Adams
Letter to Elbridge Gerry May 20, 1774

I have just time to acquaint you that yesterday our committee of correspondence received an express from New York, with a letter from thence, dated the 15th, informing that a ship arrived there after a passage of twenty-seven days from London, because of the detested act of shutting up this [Boston's] port.

The citizens of New York resented the treatment of Boston, as a most violent and barbarous attack on the rights of all America; that the general cry was, "let the port of New York voluntarily share the fate of Boston."

The merchants were to meet on Tuesday last, and it was the general opinion that they would entirely suspend all commercial connection with Great Britain, and not supply the West Indies with hoops, staves, lumber, etc.

They hoped the merchants in this and every colony would join the action, as it was of extreme importance.

* * * * *

Sovereignty

Sovereignty is the seat and legitimacy of power.

In the early Middle Ages, the king was seen as the seat of sovereignty – The Sovereign. But as the "Rule of Law" began (with John of Salisbury), sovereignty was more and more seated in the law. A prince was made legitimate by upholding the law, or bad by not upholding the law. This was especially true in England, where several kings specifically agreed that they would do nothing against the customs or law of the land. By the 18th Century, the most thoughtful people were concluding that sovereignty was or should be seated in the people... that God was the great and true sovereign, and that by creating man in his image, he extended his sovereignty directly (and only) to them.

Samuel Adams
Boston Gazette, January 21, 1771
The body of the people - no contemptible multitude - for whose sake government is instituted; or rather, who have themselves erected it, solely for their own good - to whom even kings and all in subordination to them, are, strictly speaking, servants and not masters.

* * * * *

In the following quote Samuel Adams is correcting John Adams, who is then Vice President of the United States. This is an excellent view into the character of Sam Adams, who stands like a rock on his principles, and corrects John Adams, who seems overtaken by the position of power he now holds. This tendency of the younger Adams (they were second cousins) was also displayed in his promotion of the Alien & Sedition Acts and other over-reaches while he was President a few years after. It was a primary cause of his break with Jefferson, a break that they fortunately mended late in their lives.

Samuel Adams

Letter to John Adams November 25, 1790

A Republic, you tell me, is a Government in which "the People have an essential share in the sovereignty."

Is not the whole sovereignty, my friend, essentially in the People?

Is not Government designed for the Welfare and happiness of all the People? And is it not the uncontrollable essential right of the People to amend, and alter, or annul their Constitution, and frame a new one, whenever they shall think it will better promote their own welfare, and happiness?

* * * * *

Standing Armies

The founders were continually concerned with standing (permanent) armies, for reasons that Sam Adams explains below. Military tactics and necessities have repetitively changed since the time of the revolution, but the subjects of Adams' concern have changed less.

Samuel Adams

Letter to James Warren January 7, 1776

A standing Army, however necessary it may be at some times, is always dangerous to the Liberties of the People.

Soldiers are apt to consider themselves as a Body distinct from the rest of the Citizens. They have their Arms always in their hands. Their Rules and their Discipline is severe. They soon become attached to their officers and disposed to yield implicit Obedience to their Commands. Such a Power should be watched with a jealous Eye.

I have a good Opinion of the principal officers of our Army. I esteem them as Patriots as well as Soldiers. But if this War continues, as it may for years yet to come, we know not who may succeed them. Men who have been long subject to military Laws and inured to military Customs and Habits, may lose the Spirit and Feeling of Citizens.

And even Citizens, having been used to admire the Heroism which the Commanders of their own Army have displayed, and to look up to them as their Saviors may be prevailed upon to surrender to them those Rights for the protection of which against Invaders they had employed and paid them. We have seen too much of this Disposition among some of our Countrymen.

The Militia is composed of free Citizens. There is therefore no Danger of their making use of their Power to the destruction of their own Rights, or suffering others to invade them.

I earnestly wish that young Gentlemen of a military Genius (& many such I am satisfied there are in our Colony) might be instructed in the Art of War, and at the same time taught the Principles of a free Government, and deeply impressed with a Sense of the indispensable Obligation which every member is under to the whole Society. These might be in time fit for officers in the Militia, and being thoroughly acquainted with the Duties of Citizens as well as soldiers, might Command of our Army at such times as Necessity might require so dangerous a Body to exist.

* * * * *

The States, Powers Of

While people often use the term "state's rights," the states, under the US Constitution, are given or forbidden "powers." Rights exist in the people and are inalienable.

James Madison
Federalist #25

The powers delegated by the proposed Constitution to the federal government are few and defined. Those which are to remain in the State governments are numerous and indefinite.

The former [central government powers] will be exercised principally on external objects, as war, peace, negotiation and foreign commerce.

The powers reserved to the several States will extend to all the objects which in the ordinary course of affairs, concern the lives and liberties, and properties of the people, and the internal order, improvement and prosperity of the State.

As in many other places, "several" means "separate."

* * * * *

Madison, the primary author of the Constitution, clarifies that the states have the duty to interpose – that is, to place themselves as a protective barrier – to protect the people from the evils of the federal government. No tame words here!

James Madison
Virginia Resolution of 1798

This Assembly doth explicitly and peremptorily declare, that it views the powers of the federal government, as resulting from the compact, to which the states are parties, as limited by the plain sense and intention of the instrument constituting the compact; as no further valid than they are authorized by the grants enumerated in that compact; and that in case of deliberate, palpable, and dangerous exercise of other powers, not granted by the said compact, the states who are parties thereto, have the right, and are in duty bound, to interpose, for arresting the progress of the evil, and for maintaining within their respective limits, the authorities, rights and liberties appertaining to them.

* * * * *

Thomas Jefferson
Letter to William Johnson, 1823
The capital and leading object of the Constitution was to leave with the States all authorities which respected their own citizens only, and to transfer to the United States those which respected citizens of foreign or other States; to make us several [separate] as to ourselves, but one as to all others.

* * * * *

Status

In England, Europe, and most of the world, the status of birth and class were important. This affected life in the colonies as well, but status faded in America over time, as merit overtook accidents of birth as the characteristics that mattered.

Benjamin Franklin
Information to Those Who Would Remove to America September 1782
Much less is it advisable for a Person to go thither [to America], who has no other Quality to recommend him but his Birth. In Europe it has indeed its Value; but it is a Commodity that cannot be carried to a worse Market than that of America, where people do not inquire concerning a Stranger, What is he? but, What can he do?

* * * * *

Here Hamilton displays a preference for the English, aristocratic structure. He believes that the rich and well-born are better people and can be trusted with more power.

Alexander Hamilton
Debates for The Federal Constitution June 18, 1787

All communities divide themselves into the few and the many. The first are the rich and wellborn, the other the mass of the people...The people are turbulent and changing; they seldom judge or determine right.

Give therefore to the first class a distinct, permanent share in the government. They will check the unsteadiness of the second, and as they cannot receive any advantage by a change, they therefore will ever maintain good government.

* * * * *

Studies

Here Adams explains that circumstances have forced him into the study of government, and that he hopes his sons can study mathematics, history and commerce, and that his grandchildren may be free to study arts.

John Adams
Letter to his wife May 12, 1780

The science of government it is my duty to study, more than all other sciences; the arts of legislation and administration and negotiation ought to take the place of, indeed exclude, in a manner, all other arts. I must study politics and war, that our sons may have liberty to study mathematics and philosophy. Our sons ought to study mathematics and philosophy, geography, natural history and naval architecture, navigation, commerce and agriculture in order to give their children a right to study painting, poetry, music, architecture, statuary, tapestry and porcelain.

Submission, Servility

To the founders, willing servility and submission were offenses against human nature, and against the Creator who formed man as an intelligent creature of free will.

Samuel Adams
Boston Gazette, October 14, 1771

The truth is, All might be free if they valued freedom, and defended it as they ought.

Is it possible that millions could be enslaved by a few, which is a notorious fact, if all possessed the independent spirit of Brutus, who to his immortal honor, expelled the proud Tyrant of Rome, and his "royal and rebellious race?"

If therefore a people will not be free; if they have not virtue enough to maintain their liberty against a presumptuous invader, they deserve no pity, and are to be treated with contempt and disgrace.

* * * * *

Samuel Adams
Boston Gazette, October 7, 1771

Let the ministry who have stripped us of our property and liberty, deprive us of our understanding too; that unconscious of what we have been or are, and ungoaded by tormenting reflections, we may tamely bow down our necks, with all the stupid serenity of servitude, to any drudgery which our lords and masters may please to command.

* * * * *

Samuel Adams

Boston Gazette, December 2, 1771

No methods are yet left untried by the writers on the side of the ministry, to persuade this People that the best way to get rid of our Grievances is to submit to them.

* * * * *

Samuel Adams

Letter to his wife December 19, 1776

Great Britain has taught us what to expect from Submission to its Power. No People ever more tamely surrendered than of that Part of the Jerseys through which the Enemy marched. No opposition was made. And yet the grossest Insults have been offered to them, and the rude Soldiery have been suffered to perpetrate Deeds more horrid than Murder.

If Heaven punishes Communities for their Vices, how harsh must be the Punishment of that Community who think the Rights of human Nature not worth struggling for and who patiently submit to Tyranny.

One week later, Adams writes to his wife that, "We are now informed that the People of Jersey & Pennsylvania are in Possession of their Understanding and that they are turning out in great Numbers to the Assistance of General Washington."

* * * * *

Samuel Adams

Boston Gazette, January 21, 1771

Philanthrop [another writer], I think, speaks somewhat unintelligibly, when he tells us that the well being and happiness of the whole depends upon subordination; as if mankind submitted to government for the sake of being subordinate:

In the state of nature there was subordination: The weaker was by force made to bow down to the more powerful. This is still the unhappy lot of a great part of the world, under government: So, among the brutal herd, the strongest horns are the strongest laws.

Mankind have entered into political societies [relationships], rather for the sake of restoring equality; the lack of which, in the state of nature, made existence uncomfortable and even dangerous.

I am not of levelling principles: But I am apt to think that the constitution of civil government which admits equality in the most extensive degree, consistent with the true design of government, is the best; and I am of this opinion, because I agree with Philanthrop and many others, that man is a social animal.

Subordination is necessary to promote the purposes of government; the grand design of which is that men might enjoy a greater share of the blessings resulting from that social nature, and those rational powers, with which indulgent Heaven has endowed us, than they could in the state of nature:

But, there is a degree of subordination, which will forever be abhorrent to the generous mind; when it is extended to the very borders, if not within the bounds of slavery: A subordination, which is so far from conducing "to the welfare and happiness of the whole," that it necessarily involves the idea of that worst of all the evils of this life, a tyranny: An abject servility, which instead of "being essential to our existence as a people," disgraces the human nature, and sinks it to that of the most despicable brute.

When Adams speaks of "leveling principles" he is referring to the "levelers" of 17th Century England who demanded equality, freeborn rights, and the elimination of privilege, as well as other specific political goals.

* * * * *

Samuel Adams
Boston Gazette, August 19, 1771
There have been, says the celebrated American Farmer, in every age and in every country bad men: Men who either hold or expect to hold certain advantages by being examples of servility to their countrymen: Who are trained to the employment, or self-taught by a natural versatility of genius,

to serve as decoys for drawing the innocent and unwary into snares.

It is not to be doubted but that such men will diligently act on this and every like occasion, to spread the infection of their meanness as far as they can...

This is their method of recommending themselves to their patrons. They act consistently in a bad cause. They run well in a mean race.

In these cases, "mean" or "meanness" refers to "morally low."

* * * * *

Samuel Adams
Boston Gazette, September 9, 1771
At present we have the remedy in our own hands; we can easily avoid paying the tribute, by abstaining from the use of those articles by which it is extorted from us.

And further, we can look upon our haughty imperious taskmasters, and all those who are sent here to aid and abet them, together with those sons of servility, who from very false notions of politeness can seek and court opportunities of cringing and fawning at their feet; of whom, through favor, there are but few among us.

We may look down upon all these, with that sovereign contempt and indignation with which those who feel their own dignity and freedom will for ever view the men who would attempt to reduce them to the disgraceful state of slavery.

* * * * *

Samuel Adams
Boston Gazette, September 30, 1771
What can be intended by all the fair promises made to us by tools and sycophants, but to lull us into that quietude and sleep by which slavery is always preceded?

* * * * *

Success

George Washington
Letter to James Anderson, December 10, 1799
Time is of more importance than is generally imagined.

* * * * *

George Washington
Letter to James Anderson, December 21, 1797
The man who does not estimate time as money will forever miscalculate; for although the latter is not paid for the former, it is nevertheless a sure item in the cost of any undertaking.

* * * * *

George Washington
Letter to George Washington Parke Custis, November 13, 1796
Rise early, that by habit it may become familiar, agreeable, healthy, and profitable. It may, for a while, be irksome to do this, but that will wear off; and the practice will produce a rich harvest forever thereafter; whether in public or private walks of life.

* * * * *

George Washington
Letter to Thomas Law, May 7, 1798
It has been a maxim with me from early life, never to undertake anything without perceiving a door to the accomplishment, in a reasonable time and with my own resources.

* * * * *

Thomas Jefferson
Letter to Peter Carr August 10, 1787
Above all things, lose no occasion of exercising your dispositions to be grateful, to be generous, to be charitable, to be humane, to be true, just, firm, orderly, courageous, &c. Consider every act of this kind, as an exercise which will strengthen your moral faculties and increase your worth.

* * * * *

George Mason
Letter to his son John June 12, 1788
Attend with Diligence and strict Integrity to the Interest of your Correspondents and enter into no Engagements which you have not the almost certain Means of performing.

* * * * *

Benjamin Franklin
Advice to a Young Tradesman 1748
Remember that time is money.

* * * * *

George Washington
Letter to George Washington Parke Custis January 7, 1798
Rise early, that by habit it may become familiar, agreeable, healthy, and profitable. It may, for a while, be irksome to do this, but that will wear off; and the practice will produce a rich harvest forever thereafter; whether in public or private walks of life.

* * * * *

Benjamin Franklin
His Autobiography (margin), 1774
Nothing so likely to make a man's fortune as virtue.

* * * * *

Benjamin Franklin
Poor Richard's Almanac
If you'd be wealthy, think of saving, more than of getting.

* * * * *

Benjamin Franklin
Poor Richard's Almanac
He who goes borrowing, goes sorrowing.

* * * * *

Suffrage

The founders did not intend suffrage – the right to vote – to be universal. Knowing that there would be a tendency for people to vote themselves money from the public treasury, they limited voting to people who had, in modern terms, "a stake in the game."

George Mason
Virginia Declaration of Rights 1776
All men, having sufficient evidence of permanent common interest with, and attachment to, the community have the right of suffrage and cannot be taxed or deprived of their property for public uses without their own consent or that of their representatives so elected, nor bound by any law to which they have not, in like manner, assented, for the public good.

* * * * *

Supervising Men

Washington had spent decades supervising thousands of men, through the most difficult circumstances. His advice in this area carries real weight.

George Washington
Letter to Col. William Woodford, November 10, 1775
Require nothing unreasonable of your officers and men, but see that whatever is required be punctually complied with. Reward and punish every man according to his merit, without partiality or prejudice; hear his complaints; if well founded, redress them; if otherwise, discourage them, in order to prevent frivolous ones. Discourage vice in every shape, and impress upon the mind of every man, from the first to the lowest, the importance of the cause, and what it is they are contending for.

* * * * *

George Washington
Letter to James McHenry August 10, 1798
It is infinitely better to have a few good men than many indifferent ones.

* * * * *

Tactics Against Free Men

In the early years of the American revolt, Samuel Adams prominently stood against all manner of manipulations and intellectual tricks to subvert the cause. He wrote many articles in the newspapers of Boston, countering one attempt after another.

Samuel Adams
Letter to William Checkley June 1, 1774
The infamous Tools of Power are holding up the picture of Want and Misery; but in vain do they think to intimidate us; the Virtue of our Ancestors inspires us--they were contented with Clams and Mussels.

For my part, I have been familiar with poverty; and however disagreeable a Companion she may be thought to be by the affluent and luxurious who never were acquainted with her, I can live happily with her the remainder of my days, if I can thereby contribute to the Redemption of my Country.

* * * * *

Samuel Adams
Letter to James Warren October 13, 1778
It is the old Game of mischievous Men to strike at the Characters of the good and the great, in order to lessen the Weight of their Example and Influence.

* * * * *

Samuel Adams
Letter to Arthur Lee January 14th, 1772
The grand design of our adversaries is to lull us into security, and make us comfortable while the acts remain in force, which would prove fatal to us.

* * * * *

Samuel Adams

Boston Gazette, December 31, 1770

Arts have been used, and are being used, to detach the rest of the Colonies from this Province; and the same arts are every day practiced, to divide the Towns in this Province from the Capital. It is the Machiavellian Doctrine, Divide et impera - Divide and Rule: But the people of this Province and of this Continent are too wise, and they are lately become too experienced, to be caught in such a snare. While their common Rights are invaded, they will consider themselves, as embarked in the same bottom: And that Union which they have hitherto maintained, against all the Efforts of their more powerful common Enemies, will remain cemented, notwithstanding such trifling letter writers as these.

* * * * *

Samuel Adams

Boston Gazette, December 9, 1771

When designs are formed to raze the very foundation of a free government, whose few who are to erect their grandeur and fortunes upon the general ruin, will employ every art to sooth the devoted people into a state of indolence, inattention and security, which is forever the fore-runner of slavery.

"Indolence" means numbness, laziness or sloth.

* * * * *

Taxes

Adams resents, not just the excessive taxes, but that more and more regulators and tax agents are being sent upon them – and that the more officers that must be fed from their taxes, the more taxes will have to rise and the more aggressively they will have to be enforced.

Samuel Adams
Boston Gazette, July 29, 1771
We severely feel the effects, not of a revenue raised, but a tribute extorted, without our free consent or control.

Pensioners and Placemen are daily multiplying; and fleets and standing armies posted in North America, for no other apparent or real purpose, than to protect the exactors and collectors of the tribute; for which they are to be maintained, & many of them in pomp & pride to triumph over and insult an injured people, and suppress if possible, even their murmurs. And there is reason to expect, that the continual increase of their numbers will lead to a proportional increase of a tribute to support them.

What would be the consequence? Either on the one hand, an abject slavery in the people, which is ever to be deprecated; or, a determined resolution, openly to assert and maintain their rights, liberties and privileges. The effects of such a resolution may for some time be retarded by flattering hopes and prospects; and while it is the duty of all persons of influence here to inculcate the sentiments of moderation, it will in our opinion, be equally the wisdom of the British administration, to consider the danger of forcing a free people by oppressive measures into a state of desperation.

We have reason to believe that the American Colonies, however they may have disagreed among themselves in one mode of opposition to arbitrary measures, are still united in the main principles of constitutional & natural liberty; and that they will not give up one single point in contest of any importance, though they may take no violent measures to obtain them.

The taxing their property without their consent, and thus appropriating it to the purposes of their slavery and destruction, is justly considered, as contrary to and subversive of their original social compact, and their intention in uniting under it.

* * * * *

Adams and Franklin discuss the need of promptly opposing taxation, so that the people do not acquiesce. Also that they fear no officer will ever consent to roll them back after that point.

Samuel Adams
Letter to Benjamin Franklin, June 29, 1771

While an act remains in force for that purpose [taxes], and is daily put in execution; and the longer it remains the more danger there is of the people's becoming so accustomed to arbitrary and unconstitutional taxes, as to pay them without discontent; and then, as you justly observe, no Minister will ever think of taking them off, but will rather be encouraged to add others.

* * * * *

Here Samuel Adams expresses a sentiment that is very close to that of modern anti-tax people: "We pay only because we would be locked in jail otherwise. We do not consent and we consider this immoral."

Samuel Adams
Letter to Benjamin Franklin, June 29, 1771

We therefore desire it may be universally understood, that although the tribute is paid, it is not paid freely: It is extorted and torn from us against our will: We bear the insult and the injury for the present, grievous as it is, with great impatience; hoping that the wisdom and prudence of the nation will at length dictate measures consistent with natural justice and equity: For what shall happen in future, We are not answerable.

* * * * *

This is the anti-tax resolution that preceded the Boston Tea Party.

Samuel Adams
Resolutions Of The Town Of Boston, November 5, 1773
Resolved, that the disposal of their own property is the Inherent Right of Freemen; that there can be no property in that which another can of right take from us without our consent; that the Claim of Parliament to tax America, is in other words a claim of Right to buy Contributions on us at pleasure...

The Resolutions lately come by the East India Company, to send out their Teas to America Subject to the payment of Duties on its being landed here, is an open attempt to enforce the Ministerial Plan, and a violent attack upon the Liberties of America...

That whoever shall directly or indirectly countenance this attempt, or in any wise aid or abet in unloading receiving or vending the Tea sent or to be sent out by the East India Company while it remains subject to the payment of a duty here is an Enemy to America...

That a Committee be immediately chosen to wait on those Gentlemen, who it is reported are appointed by the East India Company to receive and sell said Tea, and to request them from a regard to their own characters and the peace and good order of this Town and Province immediately to resign their appointment.

* * * * *

As an old man (in the year of his death), Jefferson was back at his home and financially insolvent. In his desperation, old friends and admirers in New York sent him quite a few thousands of dollars. Here, he expresses his gratitude and his pleasure that not one cent of the money was "wrung" (twisted forcibly) from taxpayers.

Thomas Jefferson
Letter to his oldest grandson February 8, 1826
No cent is wrung from the taxpayer. It is the pure and unsolicited offering of love.

* * * * *

Franklin here expresses a counter-argument: That the losses men bring upon themselves are often worse than taxes. This is not a fully honest argument (self-losses being worse does not make other losses "okay"), but Franklin's scenario does certainly occur, and it is often a more practical thing to repair one's self, rather than to oppose (and place all blame upon) an external actor.

Benjamin Franklin
Letter to Charles Thomson July 11, 1765
Idleness and Pride Tax with a heavier Hand than Kings and Parliaments; If we can get rid of the former we may easily bear the Latter.

* * * * *

Here, during the Presidency of John Adams, Jefferson proposes a system of taxation whereby a central tax-collecting organization may be avoided. In it, the states are permitted to raise their share of the national taxes by a land tax, and that if they fail to deliver, then the central government may step in and collect the tax.

Thomas Jefferson
Letter to Peregrine Fitzhugh, 1797
I am suggesting an idea on the subject of taxation which might, perhaps, facilitate much that business, and reconcile all parties. That is to lay a land tax, leviable in 1798, and so on.

But if by the last day of 1798, any State shall bring its whole quota into the Federal Treasury, the tax shall be suspended one year for that State. If by the end of the next year they bring another year's tax, it shall be suspended a second year as to them, and so on forever.

If they fail, the Federal collectors will go on, of course, to make their collection.

In this way, those who prefer excises may raise their quota by excises, and those who prefer land taxes may raise by land taxes, either on the Federal plan, or on any other of their own which they like better.

This would tend, I think, to make the General Government popular, and to render the State Legislatures useful allies and associates instead of rivals, and to mollify the harsh tone of government which has been asserted.

I find the idea pleasing to most of those to whom I have suggested it. It will be objected to by those who are for consolidation.

* * * * *

Taxes, Evasion Of

Hamilton argues for strong national government because it is superior in preventing the evasion of taxes and regulation.

Alexander Hamilton
Federalist #12
The relative situation of these States; the number of rivers with which they are intersected, and of bays that wash there shores; the facility of communication in every direction; the affinity of language and manners; the familiar habits of intercourse; --all these are circumstances that would conspire to render an illicit trade between them a matter of little difficulty, and would insure frequent evasions of the commercial regulations of each other.

Threats

George Washington
Letter to John Jay, May 18, 1786
Ignorance and design are difficult to combat. Out of these proceed illiberal sentiments, improper jealousies, and a train of evils which oftentimes in republican governments must be sorely felt before they can be renewed.

Washington's meaning of "design" is difficult to ascertain. He probably means "structure;" as overcoming the limitations and incentives of hierarchies is an especially difficult set of problems.

* * * * *

Thomas Jefferson
Notes on the State of Virginia, 1781-1785
Can the liberties of a nation be thought secure when we have removed their only firm basis, a conviction in the minds of the people that these liberties are of the gift of God?

* * * * *

Thomas Jefferson
Opinion on creating a National Bank 1791
I consider the foundation of the Constitution as laid on this ground: That "all powers not delegated to the United States, by the Constitution, nor prohibited by it to the States, are reserved to the States or to the people." To take a single step beyond the boundaries thus specially drawn around the powers of Congress, is to take possession of a boundless field of power.

* * * * *

Truth

Thomas Jefferson
Notes on Religion October 1776
Truth.. seldom has received much aid from the power of great men to whom she is rarely known & seldom welcome.

* * * * *

Thomas Jefferson
Bill to Establish Religious Freedom 1779
[I hold that] truth is great and will prevail if left to herself; that she is the proper and sufficient antagonist to error, and has nothing to fear from the conflict unless by human interposition disarmed of her natural weapons, free argument and debate; errors ceasing to be dangerous when it is permitted freely to contradict them.

* * * * *

Patrick Henry
Second Virginia Convention March 23, 1775
Are we disposed to be of the number of those who, having eyes, see not, and, having ears, hear not, the things which so nearly concern their earthly salvation? For my part, whatever anguish of spirit it may cost, I am willing to know the whole truth; to know the worst, and to provide for it.

* * * * *

Samuel Adams
Letter to John Adams October 4, 1790
Blind opinion… is always an Enemy to truth.

* * * * *

Tyranny

It is interesting to see precisely which actions the founders defined as tyrannical.

Samuel Adams
Independent Chronicle, January 20, 1794
In this state of society, the unalienable rights of nature are held sacred, and each member is entitled to an equal share of all the social rights.

No man can rightly become possessed of a greater share: If anyone usurps it, he so far becomes a tyrant.

* * * * *

Thomas Jefferson
Bill to Establish Religious Freedom 1779
To compel a man to furnish contributions of money for the propagation of opinions which he disbelieves and abhors, is sinful and tyrannical.

* * * * *

Thomas Jefferson
Letter to Benjamin Rush September 23, 1800
I have sworn upon the altar of god eternal hostility against every form of tyranny over the mind of man.

Jefferson is not only opposed to tyranny over the bodies of men, but especially tyranny over their minds. (Which easily leads to tyranny over their bodies as well.)

* * * * *

John Adams
Defense of the Constitutions of Government 1787
The moment the idea is admitted into society, that property is not as sacred as the law of God, and that there is not a force

of law and public justice to protect it, anarchy and tyranny commence.

* * * * *

George Mason
Virginia Declaration of Rights 1776
The freedom of the press... can never be restrained, except by despotic governments.

* * * * *

Here John Adams explains that while people have every right to kill a tyrant, this will not guarantee liberty and happiness. Liberty must be specifically built in a people – the mere elimination of a tyrant does little to support it.

John Adams
Defense of the Constitutions of Government 1787
The right of a nation to kill a tyrant, in cases of necessity, can no more be doubted, than to hang a robber, or kill a flea. But killing one tyrant only makes way for worse, unless the people have sense, spirit and honesty enough to establish and support a constitution guarded at all points against the tyranny of the one, the few, and the many.

* * * * *

Vice

Benjamin Franklin
Poor Richard's Almanac
Virtue may not always make a Face handsome, but Vice will certainly make it ugly.

* * * * *

Virtue

On no subject were the Founders more clear and more in unison than that of virtue: Goodness, justice, morality, righteousness, kindness, courage, etc. They were especially convinced that the path to slavery begins with the destruction of virtues.

Samuel Adams
Letter to John Scollay April 30 1776

I have long been convinced that our Enemies have made it an Object, to eradicate from the Minds of the People in general a Sense of true Religion and Virtue, in hopes thereby the more easily to carry their Point of enslaving them. Indeed my Friend, this is a Subject so important in my Mind, that I know not how to leave it. Revelation assures us that "Righteousness exalteth a Nation"- -Communities are dealt with in this World by the wise and just Ruler of the Universe. He rewards or punishes them according to their general Character.

The diminishing of public virtue is usually attended with that of public Happiness, and the public Liberty will not long survive the total Extinction of Morals. "The Roman Empire," says the Historian, must have sunk, though the Goths had not invaded it. Why? "Because the Roman Virtue was sunk."

* * * * *

Samuel Adams
Boston Gazette, October 5, 1772

It is in the Interest of Tyrants to reduce the People to Ignorance and Vice. For they cannot live in any Country where Virtue and Knowledge prevail.

* * * * *

Samuel Adams

Boston Gazette, October 5, 1772

It is always observable, that those who are combined to destroy the People's Liberties, practice every Art to poison their Morals.

* * * * *

Samuel Adams

Letter to Elbridge Gerry October 29, 1775

After all, virtue is the surest means of securing the public liberty. I hope you will improve the golden opportunity of restoring the ancient purity of principles and manners in our country. Every thing that we do, or ought to esteem valuable, depends upon it. For freedom or slavery, says an admired writer, will prevail in a country according as the disposition and manners of the inhabitants render them fit for the one or the other.

To paraphrase Adams: Only people with virtue are fit for liberty. Those without virtue are fit only to servitude and slavery. All tend to rise or fall to their own level.

* * * * *

Samuel Adams

Letter to James Warren December 26, 1775

At present our Council as well as our House of Representatives are annually elective. Thus far they are accountable to the people, as they are liable for Misbehavior to be discarded; but this is not a sufficient Security to the People unless they are themselves Virtuous.

If we wish for "another Change," must it not be a Change of Manners? If the youth are carefully educated--If the Principles of Morality are strongly inculcated on the Minds of the People--the End and Design of Government clearly understood and the Love of our Country the ruling Passion, uncorrupted Men will then be chosen for the representatives of the People.

* * * * *

Samuel Adams

Letter to James Warren October 13, 1778

True Religion & good Morals are the only solid Foundations of public Liberty and Happiness.

* * * * *

Samuel Adams

Loyalty and Sedition, The Advertiser, 1748

He therefore is the truest friend to the liberty of his country who tries most to promote its virtue, and who, so far as his power and influence extend, will not suffer a man to be chosen into any office of power and trust who is not a wise and virtuous man.

We must not conclude merely upon a man's haranguing upon liberty, and using the charming sound, that he is fit to be trusted with the liberties of his country. It is not unfrequent to hear men declaim loudly upon liberty, who, if we may judge by the whole tenor of their actions, mean nothing else by it but their own liberty, - to oppress without control or the restraint of laws all who are poorer or weaker than themselves.

It is not, I say, unfrequent to see such instances, though at the same time I esteem it a justice due to my country to say that it is not without shining examples of the contrary kind; - examples of men of a distinguished attachment to this same liberty I have been describing; whom no hopes could draw, no terrors could drive, from steadily pursuing, in their sphere, the true interests of their country; whose fidelity has been tried in the nicest and tenderest manner, and has been ever firm and unshaken.

The sum of all is, if we would most truly enjoy this gift of Heaven, let us become a virtuous people.

* * * * *

John Adams

Letter to the Officers of the First Brigade of the Third Division of the Militia of Massachusetts October 11, 1798

We have no government armed with power capable of contending with human passions unbridled by morality and religion. Avarice, ambition, revenge, or gallantry, would break the strongest cords of our Constitution as a whale goes through a net.

Our Constitution was made only for a religious and moral people. It is wholly inadequate for the government of any other.

* * * * *

George Washington

Farewell Address September 17, 1796

Of all the dispositions and habits which lead to political prosperity, religion and morality are indispensable supports. In vain would that man claim the tribute of patriotism who should labor to subvert these great pillars of human happiness - these firmest props of the duties of men and citizens.

* * * * *

John Adams

Letter to Zabdiel Adams June 21, 1776

The only foundation of a free Constitution is pure Virtue, and if this cannot be inspired into our People in a greater Measure than they have it now, they may change their Rulers and the forms of Government, but they will not obtain a lasting Liberty. They will only exchange Tyrants and Tyrannies.

* * * * *

Benjamin Franklin

Articles of Belief and Acts of Religion 1728

I believe there is one Supreme most perfect being. ... I believe He is pleased and delights in the happiness of those He has created; and since without virtue man can have no happiness in this world, I firmly believe He delights to see me virtuous.

*****

Benjamin Franklin
Poor Richard's Almanac
Great Beauty, great strength, & great Riches, are really & truly of no great Use; a right Heart exceeds all.

*****

The Voice of God

Sam Adams, a highly religious man, here merges the voice of God with reason.

Samuel Adams
Letter to John Adams November 25, 1790
The calm Voice of Reason, which is the Voice of God

*****

Voluntaryism

Here, early in the war, Hamilton, with his immense powers of perception, describes and endorses a voluntaryist philosophy: No man has any right to special powers over others, unless the others specifically and voluntarily grant them. He goes so far as to say that without specific voluntary agreement to grant power to a ruler, no man has any obligation to obey.

Alexander Hamilton
The Farmer Refuted, 1775
The origin of all civil government, justly established, must be a voluntary compact, between the rulers and the ruled; and must be liable to such limitations, as are necessary for the

security of the absolute rights of the latter; for what original title can any man or set of men have, to govern others, except their own consent?

To usurp dominion over a people, to their annoyance, or to grasp at a more extensive power than they are willing to entrust, is to violate that law of nature, which gives every man a right to his personal liberty; and can, therefore, confer no obligation to obedience.

The original rendering of "to their annoyance" was originally "in their own despite." This usage of the word 'despite' is archaic and difficult to render in modern language.

✻ ✻ ✻ ✻ ✻

Samuel Adams
The Rights Of The Colonists November 20, 1772
All Men have a Right to remain in a State of Nature as long as they please; and in case of intolerable Oppression, Civil or Religious, to leave the Society they belong to, and enter into another.

When Men enter into Society, it is by voluntary consent.

✻ ✻ ✻ ✻ ✻

War

War has often been, as Washington says below, a sad, final alternative. And in some cases (such as that of the second quote below), valor in war is crucial even to the history of mankind. But when viewed from a small distance, as Franklin notes at the end of this section, war is also almost insane. A great many wars change little, aside from aiding certain parties and killing many others.

George Washington
Letter to George William Fairfax May 31, 1775
Unhappy it is though to reflect, that a Brother's Sword has been sheathed in a Brother's breast, and that, the once happy

and peaceful plains of America are either to be drenched with Blood, or Inhabited by Slaves. Sad alternative! But can a virtuous Man hesitate in his choice?

* * * * *

George Washington
Address to the Continental Army before the Battle of Long Island August 27, 1776
The time is now near at hand which must probably determine whether Americans are to be freemen or slaves; whether they are to have any property they can call their own; whether their houses and farms are to be pillaged and destroyed, and themselves consigned to a state of wretchedness from which no human efforts will deliver them.

The fate of unborn millions will now depend, under God, on the courage and conduct of this army. Our cruel and unrelenting enemy leaves us only the choice of brave resistance, or the most abject submission. We have, therefore, to resolve to conquer or die.

* * * * *

George Washington
Letter of Instructions to the Captains of the Virginia Regiments July 29, 1759
Discipline is the soul of an army. It makes small numbers formidable; procures success to the weak, and esteem to all.

* * * * *

Benjamin Franklin
Letter to Josiah Quincy September 11, 1783
There never was a good war or a bad peace.

* * * * *

Benjamin Franklin

Letter to Mary Hewson Jan. 27, 1783

All Wars are Follies, very expensive, and very mischievous ones. When will Mankind be convinced of this, and agree to settle their Differences by Arbitration? Were they to do it, even by the Cast of a Die, it would be better than by Fighting and destroying each other.

* * * * *

War, Enemy of Public Liberty

James Madison

Political Observations April 20, 1795

Of all the enemies to public liberty war is, perhaps, the most to be dreaded, because it comprises and develops the germ of every other.

War is the parent of armies; from these proceed debts and taxes; and armies, and debts, and taxes are the known instruments for bringing the many under the domination of the few.

In war, too, the discretionary power of the Executive is extended; its influence in dealing out offices, honors, and emoluments is multiplied; and all the means of seducing the minds, are added to those of subduing the force of the people. The same malignant aspect in republicanism may be traced in the inequality of fortunes, and the opportunities of fraud, growing out of a state of war, and in the degeneracy of manners and of morals engendered by both.

No nation could preserve its freedom in the midst of continual warfare.

* * * * *

James Madison
Letter to Thomas Jefferson May 13, 1798
Perhaps it is a universal truth that the loss of liberty at home is to be charged against provisions against danger, real or pretended from abroad.

* * * * *

War, Instrument of Domestic Tyranny

War is the health of the state because it makes the state necessary. In times of peace, the state is often resented, as Madison mentions. In time of war, however, people are willing to forget assaults on liberty: It is better to be a serf than a corpse.

James Madison
Speech at the Constitutional Convention June 29, 1787
In time of actual war, great discretionary powers are constantly given to the Executive Magistrate. Constant apprehension of War, has the same tendency to render the head too large for the body. A standing military force, with an overgrown Executive will not long be safe companions to liberty.

The means of defense against foreign danger, have been always the instruments of tyranny at home. Among the Romans it was a standing maxim to excite a war, whenever a revolt was apprehended. Throughout all Europe, the armies kept up under the pretext of defending, have enslaved the people.

* * * * *

Warrants

George Mason here precedes the fourth amendment of the US Constitution by stating that no man's rights should be transgressed, except for specific reasons and supported by specific evidence.

George Mason
Virginia Declaration of Rights 1776
General warrants, whereby any officer or messenger may be commanded to search suspected places without evidence of a fact committed, or to seize any person or persons not named, or whose offense is not particularly described and supported by evidence, are grievous and oppressive and ought not to be granted.

* * * * *

George Washington

All of the founders held a very high opinion of George Washington, as did his soldiers, who spent years with him in the most difficult of circumstances. He was trustworthy in the extreme. George Washington was a man upon whom you could rely, at any time and in complete confidence.

Franklin was wiser, Hamilton had a deeper understanding, Jefferson was more knowledgeable, Adams was more engaging, Madison was more astute, but they all held Washington in the very highest esteem, as the quotes below illustrate.

Abigail Adams
Letter to her husband (John Adams) 1789
He [Washington] is polite with dignity, affable without formality, distant without haughtiness, grave without austerity; modest, wise and good.

* * * * *

Francis Hopkinson (signer of the Declaration of Independence)

He is the best and the greatest man the world ever knew... Neither depressed by disappointment and difficulties, nor elated with a temporary success. He retreats like a General and attacks like a Hero.

* * * * *

Thomas Jefferson

Letter to Dr. Walter Jones January 2, 1814

His mind was great and powerful, without being of the very first order; his penetration strong, though, not so acute as that of a Newton, Bacon, or Locke; and as far as he saw, no judgment was ever sounder. It was slow in operation, being little aided by invention or imagination, but sure in conclusion.

* * * * *

Thomas Jefferson

Letter to Dr. Walter Jones January 2, 1814

On the whole, his character was, in its mass, perfect, in nothing bad, in few points indifferent; and it may truly be said, that never did nature and fortune combine more perfectly to make a man great, and to place him in the same constellation with whatever worthies have merited from man an everlasting remembrance ... These are my opinions of General Washington, which I would vouch at the judgment seat of God, having been formed on an acquaintance of thirty years.

High praise indeed.

* * * * *

Thomas Jefferson

Letter to Dr. Walter Jones January 2, 1814

Perhaps the strongest feature in his character was prudence, never acting until every circumstance, every consideration, was maturely weighed; refraining if he saw a doubt, but, when once decided, going through with his purpose, whatever obstacles opposed.

His integrity was most pure, his justice the most inflexible I have ever known, no motives of interest or consanguinity, of friendship or hatred, being able to bias his decision. He was, indeed, in every sense of the words, a wise, a good, and a great man.

His temper was naturally high toned; but reflection and resolution had obtained a firm and habitual ascendancy over it. If ever, however, it broke its bonds, he was most tremendous in his wrath. In his expenses he was honorable, but exact; liberal in contributions to whatever promised utility; but frowning and unyielding on all visionary projects and all unworthy calls on his charity. His heart was not warm in its affections; but he exactly calculated every man's value, and gave him a solid esteem proportioned to it.

His person, you know, was fine, his stature exactly what one would wish, his deportment easy, erect and noble; the best horseman of his age, and the most graceful figure that could be seen on horseback.

* * * * *

Ethan Allen
After the Revolution
Nothing ever made the British shit like the sight of George Washington.

* * * * *

Thomas Jefferson
Letter to W. B. Giles, 1795
He errs as other men do, but he errs with integrity.

* * * * *

Washington's Rules Of Conduct

Washington's rules of conduct have circulated from time to time. They are, however, not original with him, apparently originating in France during the late 16ᵗʰ Century. Neither is it certain how often Washington referred to these rules, although he wrote out a copy of the Rules in his school book when he was about sixteen – precisely the time when he would have been paying close attention to such things.

1. Every action done in company, ought to be with some sign of respect to those that are Present.

2. When in company, do not put your hands to any part of the body, not usually uncovered.

3. Show nothing to your friend that may frighten him.

4. In the presence of others do not sing to yourself with a humming noise, nor drum with your fingers or feet.

5. If you cough, sneeze, sigh, or yawn, do it not aloud but privately; and do not speak in your yawning, but put your handkerchief or hand before your face and turn aside.

6. Sleep not when others speak, sit not when others stand, speak not when you should hold your peace, walk not on when others stop.

7. Put not off your cloths in the presence of others, nor go out your chamber half dressed.

8. At play and at a fire its good manners to give place to the last comer, and affect not to speak louder than ordinary.

9. Spit not in the fire, nor stoop low before it; neither put your hands into the flames to warm them, nor set your feet upon the fire especially if there be food before it.

10. When you sit down, keep your feet firm and even, without putting one on the other or crossing them.

11. Shift not yourself in the sight of others nor chew your nails.

12. Shake not the head, feet, or legs roil not the eyes lift not one eyebrow higher than the other, twist not the mouth, and wet

no mans face with your spittle, by approaching too near him when you speak.

13. Kill no vermin as fleas, lice, ticks, etc. in the sight of others. If you see any filth or thick spittle put your foot dexterously upon it if it be upon the cloths of your companions, put it off privately, and if it be upon your own cloths return thanks to him who puts it off.

14. Turn not your back to others especially in speaking, do not shake the table or desk on which another reads or writes, lean not upon any one.

15. Keep your nails clean and short, also your hands and teeth clean yet without showing any great concern for them.

16. Do not puff up the cheeks, stick not out the tongue rub the hands, or beard, thrust out the lips, or bite them or keep the lips too open or too close.

17. Be no flatterer, neither play with any that delights not to be played with.

18. Read no letters, books, or papers in company but when there is a necessity for the doing of it you must ask leave: come not near the books or writings of another so as to read them unless desired or give your opinion of them unasked also look not closely when another is writing a letter.

19. Let your countenance be pleasant but in serious matters somewhat grave.

20. The gestures of the body must be suited to the discourse you are upon.

21. Reproach none for the infirmities of nature, nor delight to put them with infirmities in mind of them.

22. Do not show yourself glad at the misfortune of another, even though he be your enemy.

23. When you see a crime punished, you may be inwardly pleased; but always show pity to the suffering offender.

24. Do not laugh too loud or too much at any public spectacle.

25. Superfluous complements and all affectation of ceremony are to be avoided, yet where due they are not to be neglected.

26. In pulling off your hat to persons of distinction, as noblemen, justices, churchmen, etc., make a reverence, bowing more or less according to the custom of the better bred, and quality of the person. Amongst your equals expect not always that they should begin with you first, but to pull off the hat when there is no need is affectation, in the manner of saluting and resulting in words keep to the most usual custom.

27. It is ill manners to bid one more eminent than yourself be covered as well as not to do it to whom it's due. Likewise he that makes too much haste to put on his hat does not do well, yet he ought to put it on at the first, or at most the second time of being asked; now what is herein spoken, of qualification in behavior in saluting, ought also to be observed in taking of place, and sitting down for ceremonies without bounds is troublesome.

28. If any one come to speak to you while you are sitting, stand up though he be your inferior, and when you present seats let it be to every one according to his degree.

29. When you meet with one of greater quality than yourself, stop, and retire especially if it be at a door or any straight place to give way for him to pass.

30. In walking the highest place in most countries seems to be on the right hand therefore place yourself on the left of him whom you desire to honor: but if three walk together the middle place is the most honorable the wall is usually given to the most worthy if two walk together.

31. If any one far surpasses others, either in age, estate, or merit yet would give place to someone less than himself in his own lodging or elsewhere, the one ought not to accept it, so he on the other part should not use much earnestness nor offer it above once or twice.

32. To one that is your equal, or not much inferior you are to give the chief place in your lodging and he to whom it is offered ought at the first to refuse it but at the second to accept though not without acknowledging his own unworthiness.

33. They that are in dignity or in office have in all places precedence but whilst they are young they ought to respect those that are their equals in birth or other qualities, though they have no public charge.

34. It is good manners to prefer them to whom we speak before ourselves especially if they be above us with whom in no sort we ought to begin.

35. Let your discourse with men of business be short and comprehensive.

36. Artificers & persons of low degree ought not to use many ceremonies to lords, or others of high degree but respect and highly honor them, and those of high degree ought to treat them with affability & courtesies, without arrogance.

37. In speaking to men of quality do not lean nor look them full in the face, nor approach too near them. Keep at least a full pace from them.

38. In visiting the sick, do not play the physician if you be not knowing therein.

39. In writing or speaking, give to every person his due title according to his degree & the custom of the place.

40. Strive not with your superiors in argument, but always submit your judgment to others with modesty.

41. Undertake not to teach your equal in the art himself professes; it smells of arrogance.

42. Let thy ceremonies in courtesy be proper to the dignity of his place with whom thou converse for it is absurd to act the same with a clown and a prince.

43. Do not express joy before one sick or in pain for that contrary passion will aggravate his misery.

44. When a man does all he can though it does not succeed, do not blame him.

45. When advising or reprimanding any one, consider whether it ought to be in public or in private; immediately or at some other time, in what terms to do it & in reproving show no sign of anger but do it with all sweetness and mildness.

46. Take all admonitions thankfully in whatever time or place given but afterwards not being guilty, take a time & place convenient to let him know it that admonished.

47. Mock not nor jest at any thing of importance break [n]o jest that are sharp biting and if you deliver any thing witty and pleasant abstain from laughing thereat yourself.

48. Wherein you reprove another be beyond blame yourself; for example is more prevalent than precepts.

49. Use no reproachful language against anyone, neither curse nor revile.

50. Be not hasty to believe flying reports to the disparagement of any.

51. Wear not your clothes foul, ripped or dusty, but see that they be brushed once every day at least and take heed that you approach not to any uncleanness.

52. In your apparel be modest and endeavor to accommodate nature, rather than to procure admiration, keep to the fashion of your equals such as are civil and orderly with respect to times and places.

53. Run not in the streets, neither go too slowly nor with mouth open. Go not shaking your arms, kick not the earth with your feet, go not upon the toes, nor in a dancing fashion.

54. Play not the peacock, looking every where about you, to see if you be well decked, if your shoes fit well, if your stockings sit neatly and clothes handsomely.

55. Eat not in the streets, nor in the house, out of season.

56. Associate yourself with men of good quality if you esteem your own reputation; for it is better to be alone than in bad company.

57. In walking up and down in a house, only with one in company if he be greater than yourself, at the first give him the right hand and stop not till he does and be not the first that turns, and when you do turn let it be with your face towards him. If he be a man of great quality, walk not with

him cheek by cheek but somewhat behind him; but yet in such a manner that he may easily speak to you.

58. Let your conversation be without malice or envy, for it is a sign of a yielding and commendable nature: and in all causes of passion admit reason to govern.

59. Never express anything unbecoming, nor act against the moral rules before your inferiors.

60. Be not immodest in urging your friends to discover a secret.

61. Utter not base and frivolous things amongst serious and learned men, nor very difficult questions or subjects among the ignorant or things hard to be believed. Stuff not your discourse with sentences amongst your betters nor equals.

62. Speak not of sad things in a time of joy or at the table; speak not of melancholy things as death and wounds, and if others mention them change if you can the discourse. Tell not your dreams except to your intimate friend.

63. A man ought not to value himself of his achievements, or rare qualities of wit; much less of his riches virtue or kindred.

64. Break not a jest where none take pleasure in mirth, laugh not aloud, nor at all without occasion, deride no man's misfortune, though there seem to be some cause.

65. Speak not injurious words neither in jest nor earnest, scoff at none although they give occasion.

66. Be not forward but friendly and courteous; the first to salute. Hear and answer & be not pensive when it is a time to converse.

67. Detract not from others, neither be excessive in commanding.

68. Go not to unfamiliar places, whether you shall be welcome or not. Give no advice without being asked & when desired do it briefly.

69. If two contend together, take not the part of either unless you must; and be not obstinate in your own opinion. In things indifferent be of the major side.

70. Reprimand not the imperfections of others for that belongs to parents masters and superiors.

71. Gaze not on the marks or blemishes of others and ask not how they came. What you may speak in secret to your friend deliver not before others.

72. Speak not in an unknown language in company but in your own language and that as those of quality do and not as the vulgar; sublime matters treat seriously.

73. Think before you speak, pronounce not imperfectly nor bring out your words too hastily, but orderly & distinctly.

74. When another speaks be attentive yourself and disturb not the audience. If any hesitate in his words help him not nor prompt him without being desired, interrupt him not, nor answer him till his speech be ended.

75. In the midst of discourse ask not to what the speaker refers but if you perceive any stop because of your coming you may well entreat him gently to proceed: if a person of quality comes in while your conversing it is handsome to repeat what was said before.

76. While you are talking, point not with your finger at him of whom you discourse nor approach too near him to whom you talk, especially to his face.

77. Treat with men at fit times about business & whisper not in the company of others.

78. Make no comparisons and if any of the company be commended for any brave act of virtue, commend not another for the same.

79. Be not apt to relate news if you know not the truth thereof. In discoursing of things you have heard, name not your author. Do not reveal a secret.

80. Be not tedious in discourse or in reading unless you find the company pleased therewith.

81. Be not curious to know the affairs of others, neither approach those that speak in private.

82. Undertake not what you cannot perform but be careful to keep your promise.

83. When you deliver a matter do it without passion & with discretion, however mean the person be you do it too.

84. When your superiors talk to anybody, do not speak nor laugh.

85. In company of these of higher quality than yourself speak not till you are asked a question, then stand upright, take off your hat & answer in few words.

86. In disputes, be not so desirous to win as not to give liberty to each one to deliver his opinion and submit to the judgment of the major part, especially if they are judges of the dispute.

87. Let thy carriage be such as becomes a serious man, settled and attentive to that which is spoken. Do not contradict at every turn what others say.

88. Be not tedious in discourse, make not many digressions, nor repeat often the same manner of discourse.

89. Speak not evil of the absent for it is unjust.

90. Being set at a meal, scratch not neither spit cough or blow your nose except there is a necessity for it.

91. Make no show of taking great delight in your meal, feed not with greediness; cut your bread with a knife, lean not on the table neither find fault with what you eat.

92. Take no salt or cut bread with your knife greasy.

93. Entertaining anyone at table it is decent to present him with food. Undertake not to help others undesired by the master.

94. If you soak bread in the sauce let it be no more than what you put in your mouth at a time and blow not your broth at table but leave it till it cools of itself.

95. Put not your food to your mouth with your knife in your hand, neither spit forth the stones of any fruit pie upon a dish, nor cast anything under the table.

96. It is unbecoming to stoop much to ones food. Keep your fingers clean & when dirty wipe them on a corner of your table napkin.

97. Put not another bit into your mouth till the former be swallowed. Let not your bite be too large.

98. Drink not nor talk with your mouth full, neither gaze about you while you are a drinking.

99. Drink not too leisurely nor yet too hastily. Before and after drinking wipe your lips breath not then or ever with too great a noise, for its uncivil.

100. Cleanse not your teeth with the table cloth, napkin, fork or knife, but if others do it let it be done with a tooth pick.

101. Rinse not your mouth in the presence of others.

102. It is excessive to call upon the company to eat often. Nor do you need others every time you drink.

103. In company of your betters be not longer in eating than they are. Lay not your arm but only your hand upon the table.

104. It belongs to the chief in company to unfold his napkin and begin to eat first, but he ought then to begin on time & to dispatch with dexterity that the slowest may have time allowed him.

105. Be not angry at the table whatever happens & if you have reason to be so, show it not but on a cheerful countenance, especially if there be strangers. For good humor makes one dish of meat a feast.

106. Set not yourself at the upper of the table but if it be your due or that the master of the house will have it so, contend not, least you should trouble the company.

107. If others talk at table be attentive but talk not with food in your mouth.

108. When you speak of God or his attributes, let it be seriously & with reverence. Honor & obey your natural parents although they be poor.

109. Let your recreations be Manful not Sinful.

110. Labor to keep alive in your breast that little spark of celestial fire called Conscience.

It may be seen at many places in this list that status, "place," rank, etc. were significant concerns. (As they have been at a great many places and times in the world.) These status customs more or less died in America, but not immediately and not among all of the revolutionary generation. (Comments listed under "The Senate" show this in particular.) In modern America, similar customs do remain in that polite persons will give special treatment and place to the elderly, the most senior man or woman, to infirm persons, to the unfamiliar, or to others who are in some pertinent way less able to endure the situation at hand.

* * * * *

The West

George Washington
Letter to David Humphreys, July 25, 1785
Let the poor the needy and oppressed of the Earth, and those who want Land, resort to the fertile plains of our western country, the second land of Promise, and there dwell in peace, fulfilling the first and great commandment.

In another place, Washington says that if he were a young man, he would go west and begin there.

* * * * *

Words

We have strong needs to transfer thoughts from one to another; also to record thoughts. Our only good way to do this is with words. Words are highly useful, but they are not perfect substitutes for reality. And because these imperfect symbols are used to represent reality, they are subject to abuse.

Samuel Adams
Letter to John Pitts January 21, 1776
How strangely will the Tools of a Tyrant pervert the plain Meaning of Words!

* * * * *

John Adams
Letter to J.H. Tiffany March 31, 1819
Abuse of words has been the great instrument of sophistry and chicanery, of party, faction, and division of society.

* * * * *

Madison explains the root of the problem:

James Madison
Federalist #37
It must happen that however accurately objects may be discriminated in themselves, and however accurately the discrimination may be considered, the definition of them may be rendered inaccurate by the inaccuracy of the terms in which it is delivered. And this unavoidable inaccuracy must be greater or less, according to the complexity and novelty of the objects defined.

When the Almighty himself condescends to address mankind in their own language, his meaning, luminous as it must be, is rendered dim and doubtful by the cloudy medium through which it is communicated.

Wrong Opinions

Thomas Jefferson
Inaugural Address, March 4, 1801
Error of opinion may be tolerated where reason is left free to combat it.

* * * * *

Youth

Benjamin Franklin
Poor Richard's Almanac
An old young man, will be a young old man.

To paraphrase: If you want to be youthful in old age, be serious and "adult" as a youth.

* * * * *

**This and other great titles
are available at:**

www.veraverba.com